THE CHURCH AS A PILGRIM PEOPLE

HEBREWS–REVELATION

Scott Nash

SMYTH&HELWYS
PUBLISHING, INCORPORATED · MACON, GEORGIA

Smyth & Helwys Publishing, Inc.
6316 Peake Road
Macon, Georgia 31210-3960
1-800-747-3016
©2001 by Smyth & Helwys Publishing

The paper used in this publication meets the minimum
requirements of American National Standard for
Information Sciences— Permanence of Paper for
Printed Library Materials.
ANSI Z39.48–1984. (alk. paper)

Library of Congress Cataloging-in-Publication Data

Nash, Scott, 1953.
    The church as a pilgrim people: Hebrews-Revelation / Scott Nash.
    p. cm.
    (pbk. : alk. paper)
    1. Church—Biblical teaching.
    2. Bible. N.T. Hebrews—Criticism, interpretation, etc.
    3. Bible. N.T. Catholic Epistles—Criticism, interpretation, etc.
    4. Bible. N.T. Revelation—Criticism, interpretation, etc.
    I. Title.
    BS2775.6.C5 N37   2001
    227'.06—dc21   2001018385
                                                       CIP

ISBN 1-57312-281-5

Contents

Acknowledgments

This book began more than twenty years ago in the classrooms, offices, and halls of The Southern Baptist Theological Seminary where I learned much about the New Testament and the church from a phenomenal group of biblical scholars and teachers. Peter Rhea Jones, long-time pastor of Decatur First Baptist Church and now a professor at the McAfee School of Theology of Mercer University, deserves credit for much that I have tried to write about Hebrews here. He suggested that Bunyan's theme of pilgrimage meshed well with Hebrews and introduced me to Ernst Käsemann's development of that theme in his book, *The Wandering People of God*. George R. Beasley-Murray, who died this past year, helped us all appreciate the bizarre beauty of Revelation, as did James Blevins, who also guided me through the difficult Greek of 1 Peter. My dissertation supervisor, Harold Songer, shaped my understanding of James in his Broadman commentary. Alan Culpepper, the editor for this series, has influenced New Testament scholarship internationally through his work on the Johannine community and its writings, including the Letters of John. Frank Stagg inevitably stands behind most of my thinking about the theological importance of the New Testament, so much so that I can no longer disentangle my own ideas from those he planted in my mind long ago. Other superb teachers were also in the New Testament department then, including Wayne Ward, John Polhill, David Garland, Gerald Borchert, Roger Omanson, and from time to time the great Zurich University professor Eduard Schweizer. I consider this book to be a modest tribute to an outstanding department at a once great seminary.

I also must acknowledge my debt to Mitchell Reddish of Stetson University. He, too, is a product of the department and seminary named above. My treatment of Revelation here betrays the impact of his forthcoming commentary on that book in the *Smyth & Helwys Bible Commentary* series.

Finally, I again thank Smyth & Helwys editor Jackie Riley. She skillfully helped transform my much too late and much too long manuscript into this book.

Scott Nash

Introduction

The Church as a Pilgrim People

Taken as a group, the books in the last third of the New Testament speak of the church as a pilgrim people. One way of trying to get at the message of these books would be to treat each one individually. Here we might try to determine the setting and objective of each writing as a key to understanding what the authors intended to communicate. We might also focus on the literary character of each book, noting the overall structure and the ways the parts fit into the whole of each writing. These ways of reading these books might help us capture some sense of each book's distinctive message and would certainly be a worthwhile endeavor.

But, we can also consider the books as a canonical unit. That is, we can look at them as a group, a group that forms a distinctive part of the New Testament canon of scriptures. They are grouped in the canon as the final scriptural word about the significance of Jesus Christ. As a group, they can be viewed in terms of their different plays on a common theme, the idea of pilgrimage. From Hebrews to Revelation we have a symphony of movements playing this theme from a variety of perspectives. In a sense, each work picks up the theme and adds its own distinctive interpretation of the main theme. By listening to the different movements of these books, we gain a much fuller sense of the larger theme of pilgrimage. And, by understanding that each work is a part of a larger whole, we gain a richer perspective for reading each book.

A helpful way I have found to focus on the theme of pilgrimage in these books is to use the full title of John Bunyan's classic, *The Pilgrim's Progress*, as a guide. Bunyan's extended title was *The Pilgrim's Progress from This World to That Which Is to Come, Delivered under the Similitude of a Dream, Wherein Is Discovered the Manner of His Setting Out, His Dangerous Journey, and Safe Arrival in the Desired Country*. The last part of his title suggests three dimensions of the pilgrim life: (1) The Manner of Setting Out, (2) The Dangerous Journey, and (3) The Safe Arrival in the Desired Country. We have, then, a beginning, a middle, and an end to the adventure of pilgrimage.

The book of Hebrews, which appears first in this group, focuses on the beginning of the journey. While Hebrews deals with many subjects, its central theme is a call to pilgrimage. It is a summons to begin the journey. The books of James, 1 Peter, 2 Peter, 1 John, 2 John, 3 John, and Jude all focus on the middle part, the journey itself. They struggle with many of the dangers experienced on the way. The last book in this group, Revelation, focuses on the end. It gives a grand vision of the final destination and offers encouragement for safe arrival in the desired country.

Any journey is beset with difficulties. Fear and inertia may endanger the beginning. Pitfalls may lie along the trail threatening the journey itself. Some pitfalls may come from without in terms of wrong turns or dangerous terrain. Some pitfalls may come from within in terms of disagreement about directions or dissension among travelers. Even near the end, pilgrims may lose sight of the final destination or may despair of ever reaching it. Journeys worth making are seldom easy.

The same can be said about the journey of reading these books. Their presence in the canon involved a difficult beginning. Whereas the Gospels, Acts, and the letters of Paul early on received wide recognition among the churches, these writings were much disputed, some more than others. Questions were often raised about authorship. Who wrote Hebrews? Did Peter really write 2 Peter? Which "John" wrote Revelation? Questions were also raised about their messages. Does Hebrews teach apostasy? Does it exclude backsliders from readmission to the church? Does James have any truly Christian message, or does it actually promote a more Jewish lifestyle with a thin veneer of Christianity? Does Revelation encourage dangerous fanaticism about the Second Coming?

Such concerns about these books led many Christians and churches either to reject them outright or to use them only with extreme caution. Even after the full New Testament emerged from the debates of the fourth century, some branches of the Church continued to hold a few of these books at arm's length. Some branches never accepted all of them. As late as the Protestant Reformation in the sixteenth century, the legitimacy of some of these books in the canon was seriously debated.

Even when these books have been firmly accepted as valid scripture, the difficulty of reading them has not been resolved. In comparison to other New Testament books, they have been sorely neglected. Far more commentaries and sermons exist on the rest of the New Testament than on these writings. Partly this neglect has been due to the sense that these writings do not address the central facets of the Christian message. Whenever great attention has been devoted to these books, it has often been by fringe groups who have found support for their peculiar beliefs mainly in these otherwise neglected books. Revelation, in particular, has spawned so many unusual ideas about the Second Coming that more mainstream Christians have tended to avoid the book, not out of disrespect but out of fear for what it might say.

Thankfully, we have these books in the canon, and to ignore them or avoid them is to miss an important part of the total New Testament story. These books mark that point in the story where we, the readers, take up the challenge to enter the story ourselves. They alert us to our own struggles on the way and show us ways we can confront the dangers of pilgrimage. To take the time to read and try to understand these books is to respond faithfully to our own call to be pilgrims.

Chapter 1

Hebrews
The Call to Pilgrimage

Introduction

THE MYSTIQUE OF HEBREWS

The book of Hebrews has contributed much to the Church's understanding of who Christ is and what it means to follow him. In the
early centuries of Christianity, when the Church was developing
creedal statements that tried to express what Christians believed about
the relationship between the Father, the Son, and the Holy Spirit,
Hebrews helped the Church clarify its belief about the nature of
Christ. Hebrews affirms both the full divinity and full humanity of
Christ. To affirm both is something of a mysterious paradox, but it is a
paradox that has remained at the center of all Christian theology. In
Hebrews this mystery is fully embraced in the "Son who radiates the
glory of God and bears the very stamp of God's nature" (1:3) and the
one who was "made like his brothers (and sisters) in every way"
(2:17). The importance of Hebrews in enabling us to hold together the
two parts of this paradox cannot be minimized.

Despite its important role in helping the Church frame its theology, Hebrews is a book of mysterious origin. We know very little about
how it came to be. Hebrews has been compared to a medieval stained-
glass window, whose beauty is obvious but whose details are
mystifying. Hebrews casts a brilliant light, but the book itself is baf-
fling. Our lack of information about the kinds of things we normally
look to for help in interpretation only contributes to the mystique of
this wonderful book.

The superscription attached to the writing by the later church
epitomizes this mystique. The King James Version follows tradition in
entitling this book "The Epistle of Paul to the Hebrews." Each aspect
of this traditional title, "The Epistle . . . of Paul . . . to the Hebrews,"
contains questionable assertions.

THE EPISTLE . . .

Hebrews does not look like an epistle, or a letter. Ancient letters, including the ones in the New Testament, typically contained certain standard elements. Hebrews lacks nearly all of these elements. It does not have the kind of formal letter opening found in all the letters of Paul. Not does it have a thanksgiving or prayer section after the opening section. The body of this book lacks the typical phrases used by ancient letter writers. Furthermore, the typical pattern of Paul's letters, wherein he first generally dealt with more theological matters before going on to treat ethical issues, is lacking in Hebrews. Even the ending, which does resemble a letter, seems to be unrelated to the rest of the writing and is thought by many interpreters to be a later addition either by the author or by someone else.

Hebrews calls itself a "word of exhortation" (13:22), and that is what it seems to be. But what kind of exhortation? It reads more like an exhortatory sermon than anything else. Hebrews seems to be a homily on an assortment of Old Testament texts. The author moves from expounding on each of the texts to application of the texts to the experience of the readers; then the author moves on to other texts and repeats the cycle of exposition and exhortation. One can easily imagine Hebrews being preached. Unfortunately, we do not know enough about the nature of early Christian sermons to conclude that Hebrews was intended to be a sermon. Among the writings in the New Testament, Hebrews stands in a class by itself.

. . . OF PAUL . . .

The writing does not in itself claim to be written by Paul. It certainly differs remarkably from the known letters by Paul, not only in form but also in substance. A few people in the early church believed that Paul wrote it, but opinion was divided. Churches in the eastern part of the Christian world tended to be more open to the possibility of Pauline authorship than did churches in the West. Notable eastern scholars, however, such as Clement and Origen in Alexandria, Egypt, expressed reservations in the early third century about Paul's having written the letter as it stands. In the West, the early resistance to Pauline authorship continued to be strong until the fifth century when the respected opinions of Augustine and Jerome won Hebrews wide acceptance as a Pauline letter. The question of authorship was again raised by Reformation scholars, who, steeped in the theology of Paul, considered Hebrews to be deficient in what they held to be central Pauline themes. Since then, the consensus has developed, for various reasons, among Pauline scholars that Hebrews is not by the apostle Paul.

Several other known New Testament persons have been suggested as the author. Barnabas, whom Acts describes as a Levite from Cyprus and traveling companion of Paul, was championed near the end of the second century by Tertullian. Paul's criticism of Barnabas in Galatians over his acquiescence to pressure from devout kosher law-keepers "from James," however, makes him an unlikely candidate given Hebrews' low regard for such matters. Barnabas would had to have changed dramatically to have written Hebrews.

Because of some philosophical ideas in Hebrews that resemble the thought of Hellenistic Jewish writers such as Philo of Alexandria, some commentators believe that it was written there. Also, the approach to the Old Testament followed by Philo and many later Christian biblical interpreters in Alexandria appears to be at work in certain sections of Hebrews, especially in its treatment of certain Old Testament stories as allegories. Thus, some interpreters have followed Martin Luther's suggestion that Apollos, an eloquent Alexandrian Jewish Christian (according to Acts), wrote the letter.

If a consensus exists at all about the authorship of Hebrews today, it is that the author was "someone like Apollos." Origen, a third-century Christian scholar from Alexandria, did an extensive study of the style and thought of Hebrews and concluded that "only God knows" who wrote it. His opinion is still probably the wisest one.

. . . TO THE HEBREWS

Early in its history this writing was labeled "To the Hebrews," apparently because of its numerous allusions to the Old Testament temple cultic system. The thinking was that only people steeped in Judaism would have found the message intelligible. Paul, himself, however, in his letters to gentile Christians shows that one did not have to be a Jew or Jewish Christian to be familiar with the teachings of the Jewish scriptures. All early Christians, Jewish and gentile, considered the sacred writings of the Jewish heritage to be authoritative guides for understanding what God had done in Jesus. Certain features of Hebrews, in fact, might have been even more appropriate for a gentile audience than for a Jewish one.

The writing itself does not say to whom it was written, and the traditional title probably only reflects an early attempt to fill this gap in our knowledge. The first readers appear to have been Christians who were possibly facing persecution, but when and where or to what extent are unknown. They may also have been tempted to hide under the protective umbrella of being seen as Jews, since Judaism was generally more tolerated in Roman society than were suspicious-looking new religions. Whenever and wherever Christianity was distinguished from Judaism, it tended to be viewed with suspicion. The readers also may have grown tired and lax in their faith in the face of hardships or from pressure by Jews or Jewish-oriented Christians to defend their faith. They may also have faced the strain of understanding their faith in the light of Jesus' anticipated but delayed return. They may simply have lost the drive to have a dynamic faith. Complacency, with its attendant tendency to compromise and accommodate, may have overtaken them.

We do not know to whom Hebrews was written, by whom, or when and where. Most commentators date it around A.D. 80–100, mostly because of what seems to be a rather well developed view of Christ. It had to have been written prior to the beginning of the second century because Clement of Rome, who probably wrote at that time, made extensive use of the writing in his letter to the Corinthians.

Because Hebrews speaks of the Old Testament tabernacle and not the Jerusalem temple when it discusses the sacrificial system, some interpreters argue that the book was written after the temple was destroyed by the Romans in A.D. 70. Others contend that since the author does not use the destruction of the temple and end of the sacrificial system in his argument when it could have been his clinching piece of evidence that the old way had been superseded by a better way, the temple must have still stood. Thus, Hebrews would had to have been written prior to A.D. 70.

No argument is conclusive here. We do not know its time of writing any more than we know where, to whom, or by whom it was written. The mystique of Hebrews remains. Less mysterious, though still perplexing at times, is the book's message.

THE MESSAGE OF HEBREWS

THE STRUCTURE OF THE BOOK

Any outline of a biblical book is arbitrary. Outlines represent our attempt to present a book's message in an orderly way so that we can grasp its meaning. Often we impose our outlines on the text. Such outlines do not always match the agenda of the writer. We can never be sure that our outlines faithfully capture the thought processes at work in the writer's mind. They reflect our own thought processes as we grapple with the text. Nonetheless, for our own aid to understanding, we fashion an outline that helps the writing make sense. Many outlines have been suggested for the structure of Hebrews. None of them is perfect, but many of them are helpful. The following outline is admittedly arbitrary and imperfect, but it is ventured in an attempt to be helpful for our understanding of Hebrews.

Focusing on the theme of pilgrimage in Hebrews, we can see several structural movements. The book begins with a brilliant exordium, or introduction, that functions much as an opening fanfare does for a work of music (1:1-4). This fanfare leads into the first movement (1:5–6:20) that discusses the descent of Jesus, the Son of God, who for a while experienced the humiliation of being human. By moving from the opening description of Jesus as the glorious Son of God to his lower state as a human, Hebrews casts Jesus as a pilgrim, too. He is the pilgrim-son. In this humble, human state, he was faithful to his calling as an obedient son. Through his faithful obedience he was exalted to that heavenly sanctuary where he now serves faithfully as the great high priest. Thus, his pilgrimage took him again to the presence of the Father. This long movement has many subparts that are intricately connected to each other and to themes in the following movements.

By the time we come to chapter 7, it is clear we are in another movement. The transition into this section actually begins as early as Hebrews 4:14. In fact, Jesus' role as priest is alluded to as early as 2:17. Throughout chapters 5 and 6, however, we are still focusing on the earthly activity of Jesus that led to his exaltation. Here in chapter 7 the focus is on the priestly service of Christ in the heavenly sanctuary. This focus continues through Hebrews 10:18. The theme of priesthood developed in this movement picks up elements introduced in the first major movement. The pilgrim-son is now fully the pilgrim-priest. In this section, though, the subject of priesthood is lifted up as a sparkling jewel and examined from various vantage points. We look specifically at the kind of priesthood displayed in Christ and at the kind of priestly sacrifice he performs. For a moment, our attention is directed away from the earthly sphere to the heavenly, mindful that Christ's work in the heavenly sphere is based on what he did on earth.

In Hebrews 10:19 the focus turns to the readers, and we have passed into the final movement. The rest of the body of Hebrews retains this focus all the way through Hebrews 13:19. To be sure, the spotlight turns on the reader at specific points in the first two movements, too. Several times in the first nine chapters the author moves from his discussion of Jesus to exhort the readers to take their calling with the utmost sincerity. Beginning at Hebrews 10:19, however, the exhortation becomes primary; the writer is talking less directly about Jesus and more about those called to follow him. Earlier themes are repeated but subordinated to the persistent summons to be faithful. The vision of Christ the priest in the heavenly sphere remains before our eyes, as well as a glimpse of those great pilgrims of faith who have preceded us into the heavenly sphere (ch. 11). We are called to do faithful pilgrimage down below, but not without the assuring vision of that world toward which we journey.

Then, at the end, we have an eloquently worded benediction (13:20-21) that captures the mood of confidence the author has been seeking to build all the way through the book. This is followed by an epistolary ending (13:22-25).

An outline based on this understanding of the major movements in Hebrews would look like this:

Introduction: The Glorious Son of God (1:1-4)
First Movement: The Pilgrim-Son's Faithfulness (1:5–6:20)
    The Son Superior to the Angels (1:5–2:9)
    The Son Made Perfect through Suffering (2:10-18)
    The Son Superior to Moses (3:1-6)
    Avoiding the Faithlessness of Moses' Generation (3:7–4:13)
    The Son Appointed Priest (4:14–5:10)
    Avoiding the Danger of Sluggish Faith (5:11–6:20)
Second Movement: The Pilgrim-Priest's Service (7:1–10:18)
    The Nature of Christ's Priesthood (7:1-28)
    The Priestly Sacrifice of Christ (8:1–10:18)
Third Movement: The Pilgrim's Call (10:19–13:19)
    Hearing the Awesome Call (10:19-31)
    Recalling Past Faithfulness (10:32–11:40)
    Reaching toward the Future (12:1-29)
    Caring for One Another on the Way (13:1-19)
Close: The God of Pilgrims (13:20-25)
    Benediction (13:20-21)
    Epistolary Ending (13:22-25)

This working outline will guide the summary of each section that follows.

A SYNOPSIS OF THE THEMES

Hebrews presents the Christian life as a call to pilgrimage. The readers are exhorted not to give up or to grow lax in their faith. They are assured that their faith is rooted in a new covenant that God has established in Christ and, as such, is superior to any other way of life imaginable. Christ himself is the model for the life of pilgrimage, although other heroes of the Old Testament are also alluded to as champions of faith, which is defined as hope in an unseen reality (ch. 11). These ancient heroes looked forward in faith, trusting in something they did not see. Christians can also have hope because they have seen Jesus, the final and complete revelation of God (2:9). Christ now serves on the behalf of believers in the presence of God. In this service Christ is described as functioning much as did the Old Testament priests who carried out the sacrificial requirements of the

Mosaic covenant. Christ is a better priest, however, in that the covenant God has made through him is superior in every way to that of Moses because Jesus is the obedient Son of God and because his sacrifice is superior to the Mosaic sacrifices.

The author of Hebrews went to great lengths to argue for the superiority of faith in Christ over whatever alternatives the first readers may have been considering. Whether or not they were attracted to any particular alternative is unclear. Certainly, the life of Christian pilgrimage is contrasted favorably to many features of Judaism. In fact, a key word in Hebrews is "better" (Greek *kreitton*). Where the word "better" appears, it is always in some kind of juxtaposition with some aspect of Judaism. The whole work could be viewed as a long argument about the ways in which Christianity is "better" than Judaism.

Note, however, that in this argument the author did not engage in the kind of negative rhetoric that is so popular today. Hebrews does not castigate Judaism or belittle its beliefs and practices. Rather, Hebrews argues that something good has been replaced by something better. The surpassing merits of Christ and faith in him are applauded without condemning what may have appealed to the first readers as an attractive option.

The readers may, in fact, have feared persecution and may have attempted either to be seen by outsiders as members of a more acceptable Jewish group or to revert to Judaism altogether. The sharp contrast in Hebrews between the ways and means of the old covenant and the new covenant in Christ would have spoken to such a situation. The thrust of the contrast, however, is to highlight what believers would be giving up should they fail to live out their faith to the fullest. Given the nature of religious options in the ancient Mediterranean world, no better standard for comparing Christianity with a "good" religion could have been found than in Judaism. If believers could be convinced of how superior faith in Christ was even to the venerable, respected religion of the Jews, then surely they would not wish to risk missing out on what this faith had to offer. They would be persuaded to live out their faith in Christ in confidence and unwavering hope. They would be aroused to an active, vibrant life of faithful pilgrimage.

The readers are warned of the serious consequences of giving up in their pilgrimage. The author goes so far as to say that if they do give up, they cannot return to the Christian fold (6:4-6). This warning against apostasy, or "falling away," was a main reason many people in the early church did not like Hebrews, just as it is one reason some readers are troubled by Hebrews today. In the western part of the Christian world, where persecution was sometimes intense in the third century, some Christians had "lapsed," or renounced the faith. When the persecution ended, they wanted back into the church. Western church leaders agreed that they could return, but some objected to this on the basis of what they understood to be Hebrews' teaching against apostasy. For some people, the way to overcome this disagreement was to suppress the appeal to Hebrews by their opponents by questioning the authority of Hebrews altogether. As a result, acceptance of Hebrews into the New Testament canon was slow in the West and was only assured when Hebrews came to be included among the letters of Paul in the fifth century.

Whether or not the author actually thought that the readers could apostatize is unclear. The possibility is presented as a catastrophe too horrible to consider. In fact, the author expresses confidence that the readers will not make that mistake (6:9). Sluggishness in the faith is the overriding concern (6:12). Sluggishness is depicted as playing with fire. Too much is at stake to be complacent or fearful. Faithfulness, vibrant and invigorating, like the faithfulness evident in Jesus, himself, must be evident in the life of the believer. If they will follow Christ's lead, they will take pilgrimage seriously and engage in it robustly.

Few modern readers of Hebrews face the dilemma of being tempted to abandon Christianity for Judaism or some other religion. Some do, perhaps, but that is not the struggle for most modern-day Christians. Far more insidious is the temptation to hide within the safe walls of the Church or to embrace a version of Christianity that poses no threat to anyone, especially the Christian. Hebrews continues to summon such believers to something more. Hebrews calls us not to a place of safety but to a journey through the dangerous. The place and time of rest lie at the end of the journey, but we are not there yet. Rather, we are constantly "on the way." Failure to be "on the way" is to indulge in a sluggishness that endangers the journey itself. Hebrews calls us to be brave pilgrims.

Commentary

INTRODUCTION: THE GLORIOUS SON OF GOD
(1:1-4)

The opening line of Hebrews is an eloquently worded, brilliantly styled announcement of the supreme revelation of God in Christ. God is presented as a God who speaks, and God's definitive pronouncement is the message spoken in Jesus. The portrayal of God as one who speaks reminds us of Genesis 1: "And God said. . . ." Just as God spoke and called the world into existence in Genesis, God speaks again and again to call a people of faith into existence. In earlier times, this call came through the prophets. But now the call has come through God's Son. God's spoken word is powerful and compelling, as we will be reminded in Hebrews 4:12: "For the word of God is living and active." God's word is most alive and powerful in the Son, Jesus.

The subject of this opening sentence is God, but the object and focus is the Son. The language is different, but the thought is the same as what we find in the opening of the Gospel of John: "In the beginning was the word, and the word was with God, and the word was God, . . . and through him all things came to be." This Son in whom God has spoken is the "heir of all things," the one *for whom* creation was made. A sense of destiny and purpose is conveyed here. He is also the one *through whom* God made all things. Destiny and origin are intricately interwoven in Jesus, as Hebrews assures us repeatedly.

The one in whom God has spoken most clearly shares the very being of God. He radiates the glory of God, not as a mirror bouncing off light from its source but more as a beam of light shining from the source itself. The Son also is the "stamp" of God's being. The term translated "stamp" is *character*, originally an engraving term. It could be used of a reproduced image, as in the stamped image of an emperor on a coin. The idea here is that when you see Jesus, you are beholding the image of God. The full deity of Christ is clearly affirmed here. This divine Son "upholds the universe," not as the mythical Atlas holding the world in place upon his shoulders, but as the one who bears it along toward its goal. Again, destiny and purpose are prominent.

And how does the Son carry the cosmos toward its goal? By his "word of power." The one in whom God spoke also speaks powerfully. But where and how does the Son speak a powerful word? Through his faithful obedience to his calling. He made purification for sins. How? Through his death. When he had completed his task of purification, he assumed his seat beside God as the Son. This is his word of power.

Here at the beginning, then, we are told of a God who speaks powerfully and who has spoken most powerfully through the one who faithfully fulfilled his mission and is now recognized as the Son he is. Purpose, destiny, and mission are fulfilled in faithful obedience. The call of God to faithfulness is clearly stated at the outset.

FIRST MOVEMENT
THE PILGRIM-SON'S FAITHFULNESS
(1:5–6:20)

THE SON SUPERIOR TO THE ANGELS
(1:5–2:9)

The introduction flows smoothly into the first major movement, which contains the second contrast in Hebrews. The Son is a superior revelation to that brought through the prophets. He is also superior to the angels, who were never called "son" by God. A "catena," or string of prooftexts, about angels is culled from the Old Testament and expounded. Several of these texts had nothing to do with angels in their original context, but they are woven together here to frame a scriptural basis for affirming the Son's superiority. The angels function not as "son" but as ministering spirits sent forth to serve (1:14).

But why did the author consider it important to stress this superiority over angels? This downplaying of the role of angels may have been directed toward the kind of speculative worship of angels in Asia Minor that may be reflected in Colossians. Distinguishing Christ from angels may also, however, have been directed toward some in the Church who saw Christ himself as an exalted angel. Some ancient Jewish writings contain speculative discussions of the priestly role of angels. Some Christians may have viewed Jesus along those lines. To do so, in the thinking of our writer, would have compromised the unique mediatorship of Christ.

Probably two other concerns actually guide this effort to subordinate angels to the Son. One is to show that the revelation of God in Christ is not only superior to that of the prophets but also to the revelation that was considered by Jews to be the supreme revelatory act of God: the Law of Moses. While the Old Testament does not mention angels in connection with the giving of the Law on Mount Sinai, later Jewish tradition held that God transmitted the Law to Moses via angels. This tradition is reflected in Acts 7:53 and Galatians 3:19. Hebrews 2:2 assumes this tradition when it says that the message delivered by angels carried a just punishment for disobedience. In Hebrews 2:1, the author warns that the readers must not neglect the message they have heard about Jesus since it is a greater message than that contained in the Law brought by angels. This is the first warning of the book, and it stresses the catastrophic nature of "drifting away" from what God has revealed in Christ.

The other concern behind this focus on angels is to explain the necessity of Jesus becoming "lower than the angels" for a little while (2:9). The angels have their place as ministering spirits of God in the heavenly realm. For a while the Son became a pilgrim, traveling to the earthly plane where he had to accomplish his mission on behalf of humans. The author explains this by using Psalm 8:4-6. In its original context, Psalm 8 wonders at the unique place of humans in God's creation, made a little lower than God. The Hebrew word for God in Psalm 8:5 is *elohim*, which literally means "gods" but was generally used in the Old Testament as a name for God. The Greek translation of the Old Testament, the one apparently used by our author, translated *elohim* as "angels." The author also takes Psalm 8 to refer to Christ, not humans. Our writer also understands the "little" in Psalm 8:5 to refer to time and not degree. For a "little *while*" the Son became lower than the angels, even though, as the Son, everything had been put in subjection to him under his feet (Ps 8:6; Heb 2:8).

The downward pilgrimage was necessary so that the Son might "taste death for everyone" (2:9). This temporary humiliation "lower than the angels" was, however, the moment of his exaltation. He was "crowned with glory and honor *because* of the suffering of death." This is where we see his sonship and the dominion over all things that it entails. We do not actually see everything in subjection to the Son (2:8) as it was decreed by God (in Ps 8), but we do see Jesus who died and who in dying revealed his true identity as the Son (2:9). Hebrews is not saying that Jesus "earned" his sonship by dying, but rather that in his dying we can see who he is.

Since this Son who died is the "radiance of the glory of God and the stamp of God's very being" (1:3), he reveals to us the deepest truth about the nature of God as One who conquers death through death, as One who expresses power through suffering. This is the word from God declared by Jesus and attested by signs, wonders, miracles, and gifts of the spirit (2:4), a word to which we *must* pay attention (2:1).

THE SON MADE PERFECT THROUGH SUFFERING (2:10-18)

The opening lines affirm Christ's divinity. Hebrews also embraces the paradoxical counterpart of his full humanity. The Son was "perfected" in his suffering, and he has become the pioneer (*archēgos*) of those who are saved (2:10). The pioneer is a trailblazer, like Daniel Boone, who not only goes into the strange new land ahead of everyone else but who also leads the others into the new world. The pioneer is, thus, a model and an enabler.

The humanity of the pilgrim-son is stressed by insisting that he is "out of one" with those he came to sanctify (2:11). What the "one" is, is unclear; it could be God, Adam, Abraham, or something else. The point is, he is one with humanity. Since humans are mortal ("flesh and blood"), the Son became mortal, subject to mortality (2:14). He was made "like his brothers *in every respect*" (2:17). The implications of this assertion cannot be minimized or compromised. Pretending to be human or becoming "sort of" human are ruled out here. The Son became human, fully human, the same way humans are human. The ancient creeds of the Church expressed this conviction unequivocally, though modern Christians have often seen Jesus as something else.

Why did the Son have to become human? To complete his mission as Son. That mission was to deliver humans from their lifelong bondage to death (2:15). Specifically, the Son came to free humans from the "fear of death." That fear of death creates the lifelong bondage to "the one who has the power of death, the devil" (2:14).

Jesus came to set the captives free. Because he accomplished this free-dom through his own suffering and dying, he can offer sympathetic, meaningful help to those who struggle within the constraints of death-darkened life (2:18). His suffering was real; his death was real; he really knows what it means to be human.

THE SON SUPERIOR TO MOSES
(3:1-6)

As the pioneer, Christ surpasses the great foundational leader of Judaism, Moses. The author does not belittle Judaism or its greatest hero; he acknowledges Moses' important role. But he does affirm that Moses is not a son; only Christ is the Son. Moses was a faithful ser-vant in God's house (3:5), but Christ is over the household of God because he is the Son (3:6). Again, the author stresses that Jesus is more than a ministering spirit (angels) or servant (Moses). He has authority and dominion unequaled by other great players in God's drama. His role is unique. He alone is the Son who came to die. His death-conquering death reveals him to be the supreme reveler of the very nature of God.

AVOIDING THE FAITHLESSNESS OF MOSES' GENERATION
(3:7–4:13)

Jesus' great work as the pilgrim-son may be rendered of no effect if those he came to deliver do not themselves become faithful pilgrims. Just as Moses struggled with the wilderness generation of Hebrews who did not possess the Promised Land because of their unfaith, Jesus leads a people who must not be unfaithful to his lead. We are warned: "For we have become partners of Christ, *only if* we keep our initial conviction firm to the end" (3:14).

Psalm 95:7-11 provides the author with an important Old Testament text to undergird his warning. The passage talks about the faithfulness of the wilderness generation. Our writer emphasizes the second part of verse 7: "Today, if you hear his voice." He quotes this verse three times and alludes to it several other times. The author points out that when these words were spoken through David the wilderness generation had already failed to enter the promised rest because of their unbelief. The "Today," then, must refer to a time after then. The invitation is for another generation, the readers.

This invitation carries a severe warning: "What we must fear, therefore, is that, while the promise of entering his rest remains open, any one of you should be found to have missed his opportunity" (4:1). The opportunity to enter into the rest promised by God lies open. Obedient faith is the means of seizing the opportunity. Faithlessness is the sure way to miss it. "Let us, then, make every effort to enter that rest, so that no one may fall by following the old example of unbelief" (4:11).

THE SON APPOINTED PRIEST
(4:14–5:10)

The dangerous journey of faith is a possibility because the pilgrim-son who came to earth to accomplish his mission of deliverance is still at work. He has returned to his post in the heavens and has been appointed a great high priest (4:14). In his exaltation, Jesus has not forgotten his humiliation. His genuine experience of humanness has made him a sympathetic priest (4:15). He continues to identify with pilgrims who struggle in this life with the limitations and temptations of being human. "In every respect" he was tempted as we are (4:15). In one respect only, Jesus differs from us: He did not sin.

But what does it mean to say that Jesus did not sin in the face of temptation? Does it mean that he never did anything wrong? Does it mean that he never gave in to any human inclination to do something considered not right? How do we even define what is right or wrong in this context?

One obvious answer to this is that right and wrong are defined by the Law of God. For ancient Israel and for Judaism, the Law clearly defined what was right and wrong. But Jesus broke that Law. He healed on the Sabbath. He associated with sinners. He got angry and disrupted the worship of God in the temple. In the end, the Jewish protectors of God's Law branded him a blasphemer and in the name of the Law got him executed.

Keeping the Law, then, must not be the standard for Jesus' sinlessness. So what is? Hebrews tells us plainly:

> In the course of his earthly life he offered up prayers and petitions, with loud cries and tears, to God who was able to deliver him from death. Because of his devotion his prayer was heard: son though he was, he learned obedience through his sufferings, and, once *perfected*, he became the source of eternal salvation for all who obey him. (5:7-9)

For Hebrews, the sinlessness and perfection of Jesus consist not in Jesus' never having broken a rule. His sinlessness was not due to his being of a different nature than humans. Hebrews stresses he was like humans in every respect, even being tempted. His perfection was not due to his being God in the flesh. It was because in the flesh, especially in the most mortal dimension of fleshly existence, the pain of suffering and death, he was faithfully obedient to the Father's will. Jesus' sinlessness, according to Hebrews, was his faithfulness. He did not succumb to the temptation to give up, despite the loud cries and tears in which he prayed to God. He was faithful unto death. This is how he was "perfected" (5:8). Perfection was not for him an abstract quality or a given aspect of his nature. He *learned* obedience through suffering, and the culmination of his experience was perfection. This was the deepest dimension of his own pilgrimage. He passed through it faithfully and has now passed on to become the great sympathetic priest.

In the course of explaining how Jesus became our great priest, the author notes that all priests have some capacity for sympathizing with the people they serve since they are, themselves, drawn from among humans (5:1-2). These priests bear with the ignorant and erring since they are aware of their own weaknesses. They fill this important role of priests because they are called by God, just as Aaron was (5:4). Aaron enters the picture as the paradigm of Mosaic priests. Our author will return to discuss Aaron's priesthood in the second movement when the point will be that Jesus is different from such priests. Here the point is similarity. Jesus, too, was called by God (5:5). He was appointed by God to be a "priest forever, after the order of Melchizedek" (5:6). This important point is restated as the section closes (5:10). The author has more to say about this, but it must wait for a moment.

AVOIDING THE DANGER OF SLUGGISH FAITH (5:11–6:20)

Before the full implications of Jesus' priesthood can be explored, the author must issue a scathing indictment. His delay in pursuing the topic of Jesus' priesthood is caused by the readers' sluggishness: they have become slow in learning (5:11-12). They have not moved on toward maturity in faith. They are like infants needing milk instead of growing through solid food. They are still struggling with the basics of faith.

Our author wants to move on beyond the basics. Debates over Christian "fundamentals" are of no interest to him (6:1-2). Several such basics are named, not because they are the essentials of the faith but rather as examples of the kinds of elementary discussions that are consumed by and are consuming of spiritual infants. Something more is needed. "By God's grace," our author will try to move on to what matters (6:3).

The urgency of moving forward is highlighted by a stark description of what could happen to those who do not move forward. The words of Hebrews 6:4-8 have persistently produced their intended shock effect. They have also spawned endless debate and division over their meaning. Hebrews 6:4-8 is especially troublesome for those who affirm the security of the believer because it seems to warn that apostasy, or falling away from the faith, is possible. Attempts to make these verses say something else seldom do justice to what is actually said here. One could hardly find a better biblical description of Christian experience than that given here by the author: They have "once been enlightened," "tasted the heavenly gift," "shared in the Holy Spirit," and "experienced the goodness of God's word and the spiritual power of the age to come" (6:4-5). For such persons, having enjoyed all this and to fall away is for them to crucify Jesus and hold him up for ridicule (6:6). They are beyond repentance. They are like fields who have received the nourishing rain but still produce thorns and thistles; they are useless and face the fate of unproductive fields: burning (6:8).

Whether or not our author actually believed that no one who "backslides" after becoming a Christian can ever be returned to the fold is unclear. Nor is it evident that he was saying that anyone who commits apostasy was never really a Christian in the first place. What is clear is that our author understood the life of faith to be exactly that: a *life* of faith. For Hebrews, faith is a lifelong process. It is moving forward. Failure to move forward is equivalent to falling backward. Faith cannot be reduced to a "once-for-all" act of profession on the part of the believer, though it is based on a "once-for-all" act of faithfulness by Jesus. Trusting in what Jesus has accomplished and *living* out that trust constitutes authentic faith. The "living out" must be forward moving, fueled by a hope that shall be *realized* only in the end (6:11).

The author does not claim that any of those Christians in his audience have apostatized. In fact, he assures them of his confidence that they are in a "better state" than that (6:9). His rhetoric of urgency has prompted him to issue the stark warning so as to rekindle the life of faith they once had (6:10). What they once exhibited must be continually alive in them all the way to the end. Then, as with others who have shown faith and patience, they can receive the *promised* inheritance (6:12).

The promised inheritance, of which our author spoke earlier in his warning about unfaithfulness in Hebrews 3:7–4:13, now becomes an empowering incentive for moving forward. The promise is sure because God is the one who made it. It is doubly sure because God even swore an oath when the promise was first made to Abraham (6:13). What more assurance do pilgrims need? The hope is set before us. We can count on its being there when we arrive, after pilgrimage, to claim it. This hope is an anchor, safe and secure, there in the heavenly sanctuary where Jesus has gone as our forerunner (6:19-20). There the pilgrim-son has assumed his place as the pilgrim-priest, serving on our behalf, forever, after the order of Melchizedek. With the spotlight once again on Jesus, having heard the severe warning, we are called to resume our journey toward him.

SECOND MOVEMENT
THE PILGRIM-PRIEST'S SERVICE
(7:1–10:18)

THE NATURE OF CHRIST'S PRIESTHOOD
(7:1-28)

The second movement focuses on Jesus in the heavenly realm where he now functions as our great high priest. Jesus is not only a superior priest; he is also a superior kind of priest. He is a priest forever, "after the order of Melchizedek."

Melchizedek is mentioned in Genesis 14:17-24 and in Psalm 110, a royal psalm. In the Hebrew language of the Old Testament the word for king is *melek*. Since Hebrew was written without vowels, the actual spelling was M-L-K. The word for righteous is *zedek*, which would have been spelled Z-D-K Thus, the name M-L-K-Z-D-K could mean either "my king is righteous" or "Zedek is king." The author of Hebrews explains that his name can be translated to mean "king of righteousness" (7:2).

In Genesis 14:18, Melchizedek is described as the king of Salem (an old name for Jerusalem). The author of Hebrews (7:2) also points out that as king of Salem, he was the "king of peace" (Salem is also a form of *shalom*, the Hebrew word for peace). Genesis also calls Melchizedek a "priest of God Most High (*El Elyon*)." The name *El Elyon* possibly referred to the god the people of Jerusalem (Jebusites) at that time considered the highest god in their pantheon of gods. The Hebrews, or Israelites, of the Old Testament, used many names for God, but the most important name for them was *Yahweh*. (*Yahweh* is thought to be the pronunciation of the Hebrew name for God spelled *Y-H-W-H*.) *Yahweh* is the special covenant name by which Israel reverently referred to God. In several Old Testament passages, the name *El Elyon*, or simply *Elyon*, is connected to *Yahweh* as a descriptive name. *Yahweh* was for the Israelites the "God Most High."

The inhabitants of Jerusalem, over whom Melchizedek and his successors reigned as priest-kings, were later called Jebusites. In the Old Testament, names of persons and places that begin with the letters *Je* (in Hebrew *Y-H*) often signify an intended connection to *Yahweh* (*Y-H-W-H*). For example, several kings of Judah, such as Jehoiakim and Jehoiachin, who had other names, assumed the throne under a name that connected them to *Yahweh* and signified their legitimacy as kings. The Jebusites, then, in the fuller tradition of the Old Testament may be depicted as worshipers of *Yahweh* even though they were not Hebrews. Melchizedek, then, would have been seen as an early non-Israelite priest of the one true God. The book of Hebrews, obviously, does not cast him as a pagan. It assumes he was a genuine priest of God.

Interestingly, when David captured Jerusalem from the Jebusites, a new line of priests entered the religious leadership headed by a priest named Zadok (Z-D-K in Hebrew). Perhaps, rather than eliminating the old Jebusite priest-kings, David simply incorporated them into his ruling cabinet. This might help explain why Psalm 110 says, "You are a priest forever, after the order of Melchizedek." Psalm 110 is a royal psalm, one that was used in the coronation of the kings of Judah to signify their role as religious, as well as political, rulers. According to Old Testament tradition, David, Solomon, and all their successors functioned as important "priestly" leaders in the worship of Yahweh in Jerusalem. The way for this may have been partly paved by David assuming the priestly-king role that had been occupied by Melchizedek and his successors. One important function of Psalm 110, then, was to herald the king in Jerusalem as a priestly king or as a royal priest.

For the author of Hebrews, this identity of the royal, or kingly, priest "after the order of Melchizedek" is not stressed. Instead, the author picks up on another dimension in the brief episode in Genesis about Melchizedek. In Genesis 14:17-20, Abraham (called Abram at the time) met Melchizedek while returning from victory over an alliance of kings. Melchizedek provided Abraham with bread, wine, and a blessing. Abraham in turn showed honor to Melchizedek by paying him a tithe of the booty taken in battle. The bestowal of blessing by Melchizedek and his reception of a tithe from Abraham meant that Melchizedek was in some sense superior to Abraham.

Hebrews 7:10 says that since all of Abraham's descendants were present with Abraham in his loins (including Levi and, thus, Aaron and all his priestly descendants), the Aaronic priests were acknowledging Melchizedek's superiority. This argument reflects the Jewish idea that the loins of Adam contained all the seed of the human race and that the seed of all generations was passed down sequentially through each generation. From within the loins of Abraham, the Aaronic priests had recognized Melchizedek's superiority. Unlike the Aaronic priests, who received their priesthood by virtue of being born from Aaronic priests, Christ was appointed a priest by God "after the order of Melchizedek." Since Christ is that kind of priest, he, too, is superior to all Aaronic priests.

Furthermore, using Psalm 110, the writers assert that Christ's priesthood is eternal since Melchizedek was in some sense an eternal figure. Hebrews 7:3 points out that Melchizedek has no genealogy (in Genesis), no mother or father, and no "beginning of days or end of life." In some Jewish circles speculation about the mysterious Melchizedek led to the idea that he must have been translated to heaven, as was Elijah. Some Jews, and later some Christians, even believed that Melchizedek continued to function as an eternal priest in heaven. Some even identified him with the archangel Michael.

The author of Hebrews assumes that his readers know something about Melchizedek and his reputation as an eternal priestly figure. By claiming that Jesus is a priest after the order of Melchizedek, the author builds on his argument that Jesus is a completely different kind of priest from the Aaronic priests; he is a superior, eternal priest. Unlike the Aaronic priests, who are many in number because they die and have to be replaced, Jesus "continues forever" (7:24).

THE PRIESTLY SACRIFICE OF CHRIST (8:1–10:18)

In chapter 8, the author turns to consider the priestly work of Christ. In particular, he discusses the superiority of the priestly sacrifice made by Christ. The sacrifice of the priest Christ is superior to the Aaronic sacrifices because: (1) it is effective in cleansing the conscience, and (2) it is a one-time event. The effectiveness of this one-time sacrifice is, in turn, due to two important aspects of it: (1) the sacrifice seals a *new* covenant, and (2) the sacrifice was made in the *true* sanctuary. These four dimensions of Christ's priestly sacrifice are interwoven throughout this section, but we will follow each strand of the author's argument in turn.

Cleanses the Conscience

The great shortcoming of the Aaronic sacrifices, according to Hebrews, is that they did not work. At least, they did not work in regard to what really matters, the inward self or conscience (9:9). The gifts and sacrifices of the old covenant offered in the earthly sanctuary only served to help the body (9:10). The blood of goats and bulls and the ashes of the red heifer did sanctify the "flesh" under the old system (9:13). But more was needed. Something had to be done to purify the conscience. The pure sacrifice of the faithful and obedient Son accomplished this (9:14). Now, believers have been set free from dead works to serve the living God.

The importance of the inner conscience for Hebrews lies in the fact that it is "inner." The inner dimension is the true dimension. As it is with the inner sanctuary where the sacrifice of Christ was made, so it is with the inner part of the person. External sacrifices cannot penetrate to this inner dimension (10:3). The people under the old covenant were repeatedly reminded of this as the Aaronic sacrifices were offered year after year. They received no lasting relief from the burden of a guilty conscience. Unlike them, people under the new covenant can draw near to God with their consciences sprinkled clean by the blood of Christ (10:22). In the end, our author confesses to the readers that he is confident that his own conscience is clear (13:18).

A One-Time Event

The author of Hebrews stresses the effectiveness of Jesus' sacrifice of himself by insisting that, unlike other sacrifices, it was "once for all." It did not have to be repeated. The term used for "once for all" is a rare Greek word, *ephapax*. Three of its five appearances in the New Testament occur in this part of Hebrews. The first occurrence is in Hebrews 7:27, where the author states that Jesus did not have to make daily sacrifices for his own sins and for those of the people, as the Aaronic priests had to do. Instead, Jesus offered up himself "once for all," and it was sufficient. In Hebrews 9:12 he points out that Jesus entered the heavenly sanctuary "once for all" with his own blood and thereby secured an *eternal* redemption. In Hebrews 10:10 he repeats that believers have been sanctified through Jesus' "once for all" offering of himself.

Two other terms also express this idea of the singleness of Jesus' sacrifice in Hebrews. One is the more customary word for once, *apax*. In Hebrews 9:26 and 9:28, the author again stresses that Christ has appeared "once" at the end of the age to offer himself. The other term is a phrase that literally reads "unto all time." It appears in Hebrews 10:12 and 10:14. This phrase conveys the idea of a *continually* effective sacrifice. Because Christ's sacrifice is perpetually effective, it only had to be offered once.

All of this stress on the once-for-all-ness of Christ's sacrifice enlarges the contrast with the repeated offering of sacrifices by the Aaronic priests. The fact that they have to offer the sacrifices continually proves that those sacrifices were ineffective, according to Hebrews (9:25; 10:1-2, 11). Once an effective sacrifice for the forgiveness of sins has been made, no other is needed (10:18). By making this point repeatedly, the author is once again reminding the readers that they have a sure hope, a secure basis for moving forward.

Seals a New Coven0ant

The one-time sacrifice of Christ is effective because it is grounded in a new, different covenant relationship with God. Our author stresses that the priestly ministry (*leitourgia*, from which we derive the word liturgy) is superior to that of the Aaronic priests, as is the new covenant in which his ministry is grounded, because it is enacted on "better promises" (8:6).

The promises referred to here are found in Jeremiah's message about a new covenant (Jer 31:31-34). The idea of a new covenant that is everlasting is also found in Hosea 2. Both Jeremiah and Hosea recognized problems with the old covenant, or, more precisely, with Israel's capacity to live by the old covenant. Both prophets looked forward to a time when God would establish a covenant that enabled Israel truly to be the people they were called to be. Jeremiah affirmed that this new covenant would be an inward one "written on their hearts." Ezekiel carried the idea a step further in proclaiming that God would give the people a "new heart" (Ezek 11:19). Hebrews affirms the arrival of the longed-for covenant.

The image of a new covenant written in the heart connects with both the theme of a cleansed conscience and the theme of an eternally effective sacrifice. The old covenant sacrifices could not produce the inward experience of forgiveness, our author says (9:9; 10:4, 11). The new covenant sacrifice could and did (9:14, 15; 10:14). As mediator of the new covenant, Christ has offered a sacrifice that covers the deficiencies of the old covenant (9:15). By his death, a one-time sacrificial offering, the problem of sin is effectively resolved forever (9:26).

The death of Christ was necessitated by the establishment of the new covenant and was the means by which God established it. The writer points out that in the old covenant the shedding of blood was necessary to enact whatever external purification could be achieved (9:22). The shedding of blood meant the giving of life, and the seriousness of sin required that something of life itself had to be given to remove it. The author plays on the dual meaning of the word for covenant (*diathēkē*) to argue this point. The word can also mean "will," as in "last will and testament." Such a will is effective only upon death (9:16). The new will (covenant) God promised through Jeremiah has now become effective through a death, the self-sacrifice of Jesus (9:15).

Made in the True Sanctuary

The reason Christ's sacrifice could accomplish the forgiveness of sins through the new covenant was that it was offered where it really counted: in the true heavenly sanctuary. The author affirms this at the beginning of this section (8:1-2) and at several points throughout (9:11-12, 24). This conviction also undergirds the passionate exhortation that begins the third movement (10:19-22).

The author's argument is simple, but it involves a complex world view. In language reminiscent of the Greek philosopher Plato, Hebrews distinguishes between the really "real" in heaven and the apparently real "copy" on earth. Plato taught that all earthly forms are representations of immaterial forms or "ideas" in the heavenly realm. The problem of humanity, according to this view, is that we mistake the earthly forms for the real thing. Jewish writers influenced by Greek philosophy, such as Philo, often interpreted Old Testament descriptions of the tabernacle in Platonic terms. The various parts of the tabernacle were understood to be earthly representations of eternal concepts, such as virtue, wisdom, or the soul.

The idea that an earthly temple in some sense reflects a heavenly copy, however, was earlier than Plato and was pervasive throughout the ancient world. Most ancient cultures understood that their temples and their systems of worship mirrored a true temple in some kind of heavenly realm. The temple was the place where heaven and earth came together. In the book of Exodus, where Moses was given the instructions on Mount Sinai about the construction of the tabernacle, he was told: "See that you make them (all the objects associated with the tabernacle) after the pattern for them that is being shown you on the mountain" (Exod 25:40). Several Jewish writings from the Persian and Hellenistic periods (roughly 5th and 4th centuries B.C.) refer to this passage in depicting the tabernacle and the Jerusalem temple as copies of the true heavenly one. Hebrews 8:5 cites the Exodus passage in explaining that the earthly tabernacle was but a copy of the one in heaven shown to Moses on the mountain.

For Hebrews, the idea that the earthly tabernacle was only a shadow of the true sanctuary in heaven is crucial in explaining why the death of Christ was an effective sacrifice. Since the tabernacle was merely a copy, its sacrificial system was inadequate. In a sense, it was not real. Its purpose was to point upward to the true sanctuary and forward to the time when the true sacrifice would be made. Christ's sacrifice, however, occurred in the real heavenly temple. Heaven and earth converge not in the Jerusalem temple, but in the cross. In his death, Christ entered once and for all into the true Holy Place to present the sacrifice of his blood (9:12). Thus, the longed-for deliverance, foreshadowed and anticipated by the tabernacle/temple sacrifices, finally took place. The pilgrim-son accomplished his mission and became the pilgrim-priest in the heavenly sanctuary where he still performs his priestly service, not by offering more sacrifices but by bringing people into the presence of God.

THIRD MOVEMENT
THE PILGRIM'S CALL
(10:19–13:19)

The final major movement in Hebrews marks a transition from a focus on Jesus the pilgrim-son who has become the pilgrim-priest to those who are called to be faithful pilgrims following on the trail he has blazed. The section 10:19-39 forms a powerful exhortation calling believers to faithfulness. The first part of this unit, 10:19-31, looks back to the work of Christ. The second part, 10:32-39, looks forward to the way of faith that now lies open to pilgrims. It calls the readers to reflect on their own experience and then connects that experience to a long list of biblical persons whose journey has reached its conclusion (11:1-40). The readers are then urged to move forward (12:1-29), keeping in mind the care for one another that is called for on the way (13:1-19).

HEARING THE AWESOME CALL
(10:19-31)

Three calls begin this section: (1) "Let us draw near" (10:22), (2) "Let us hold fast" (10:23), and (3) "Let us consider" (10:24). These exhortations are followed by a stern warning (10:26-31).

The first exhortation to draw near is grounded in two realities now possessed by the faithful: (1) confidence to enter the sanctuary (10:19) and (2) a great high priest (10:21). The confidence to enter the sanctuary, the presence of God, comes from the sacrifice of Christ. This is described in two ways: (1) the blood of Christ (10:19) and (2) through his flesh (10:20). These two images speak of the same reality. Because Jesus was faithfully obedient unto death, the way into the presence of God is opened.

This is a new and living way that provides passage *through the curtain* (10:20). The curtain recalls the veil that hid the inner sanctuary of the tabernacle/temple. It marked the hiddenness and inaccessibility of God's presence. Continuing the symbolism of the previous movement, our author uses this image of the earthly curtain to depict the hiddenness of God in the heavenly sanctuary. There in that sanctuary, the real holy place of God, the way through the excluding curtain has been opened. Believers can now approach God in the true sanctuary because of what Jesus has done. Jesus is there now as the great high priest over God's household, that is, over all the people of God. He is the head of the household, and where the head is, the whole household is also present. So, they are exhorted to draw near, and to do so with a true heart in full assurance of faith (10:22).

The second exhortation is to hold fast (10:23). Specifically, we are to hold fast our "confession of hope." Hebrews will not let us forget that the way of faith is demanding. We live by hope. Confessing this hope is the beginning of possessing it, but it is not the end. We were told earlier that we do not yet see everything in subjection to him (2:8). What we do see is Jesus (2:9). We place our hope in God's promise that through the faithfulness of Jesus all things will be brought under the rule of God. Hebrews assures us that the one who has promised this is faithful; our hope is to be as unwavering as God's faithfulness.

The final exhortation is to consider how to stir up one another to love and good works (10:24). Here we have moved into the theme of this final movement. How do we live out our hope? How do we respond faithfully to the faithfulness of God in Jesus? In short, we do not do it alone. We are in this together. We must exhort one another. This involves coming together as a faith community (10:25). Our author notes that some have failed to do this. Neglecting the community of faith is dangerous, not because those who neglect are subject to excommunication, but because those who neglect have cut themselves off from the very body that can help them in their journey. Encouraging one another is vital for pilgrims, especially as the journey progresses toward the destination.

A stern warning follows these exhortations (10:26-31). It echoes previous warnings, but it is more intense. Deliberately sinning after learning the truth of God's forgiveness renders that forgiveness ineffective. It is spurning the Son of God and profaning the blood of the new covenant by which the sinner was sanctified (10:19). It outrages God's Spirit of grace. It invites severe judgment (10:27, 31). In language that later inspired Jonathan Edward's famous sermon, "Sinners in the Hands of an Angry God," the writer warns of the catastrophic consequences of not heeding the exhortations.

Was our author engaging in scare tactics? Did the author believe that God would cast out the backslider into a fury of consuming fire (10:27)? Or, is this warning to be seen as hyperbolic rhetoric designed to frighten people into faithfulness? Clear answers to such questions elude us. Clearly, the author does not take sluggishness or laxity in faith lightly. His call to full and vital faithfulness contains both positive appeal and negative caution. He exudes confidence that God is faithful. He is confident of the effectiveness of Christ's sacrifice. He also dares to express confidence that his readers will be found faithful. But, he is also alarmed that complacency has besieged at least some of his readers. Perhaps, fear has driven them to this complacency. If fear effectively directs their actions, then our author points them to a greater source of fear: the judgment of God. It is shock therapy.

RECALLING PAST FAITHFULNESS
(10:32–11:40)

The warning passes into a kinder, gentler summons. Our author recalls past faithfulness to encourage continuing faithfulness. He reminds the readers first of their own faithfulness in hard times (10:32-39). Several kinds of former suffering are called to mind: public humiliation, physical abuse, partnership with prisoners, and loss of property. The types of suffering listed resemble the afflictions of righteous people described in much ancient literature, both Greek or

Roman and Jewish or Christian writings. None of the sufferings described can be connected to a particular time or place. The experience of Christians in Rome during Nero's fanatical last years fits the description, but so might any number of other occasions in the early years of the Church. No official persecution by the Roman government is required; spontaneous, local outrages against members of a peculiar, suspicious sect would have produced the same results.

Hebrews labels these sufferings a "contest" (10:32). The athletic imagery of this term is developed later in chapter 12. Here the author focuses on the victorious way the readers competed in this contest of suffering in times past. They did so joyfully, being assured then of a reward greater than any loss (10:35). Now, they have need of the same kind of endurance, not necessarily because they must face the same kinds of sufferings but because the life of faith always calls for perseverance. The author cites Habakkuk 2:3-4, which speaks of living by faith while awaiting the deliverance of God (10:37-38). The passage also declares that God finds no pleasure in the one who "shrinks back." Hebrews affirms that those who have set out on this journey will not shrink back and be destroyed; they will keep moving forward in faith (10:39).

The writer then turns to consider the faithfulness of his readers in the larger context of the faithfulness of all God's people. Theirs is no isolated struggle. Just as they are called to reach outward to the community of faith and encourage one another, they can find encouragement by remembering the faithful lives of others in the past. The community of faith stretches through time as well as outwardly in the present moment.

The idea that faith itself has both a temporal and spatial dimension is affirmed in the first verse of the famous chapter 11: "Faith is the reality of things hoped for, the proof of things not seen." This short and deceivingly simple definition of faith is actually very complex in meaning, as can be seen in the many different attempts to translate and interpret the words given here as "reality" and "proof." Also, even though this verse can be seen as a definition of faith, we should avoid thinking that it gives *the* definition of faith. Even in Hebrews, faith can mean other things than what is stated in this verse. Overall, in Hebrews, faith has to do with faithfulness. Faith is certainly more than belief; it is primarily faithful living.

"Faith is the *reality* of things hoped for." Many translations follow the lead of Protestant reformers in understanding the Greek word *hypostasis* in a psychological sense, thus translating it "assurance." Taken this way, faith gives us a sense of assurance about our hopes. Faith may do that, but the issue is what the author of Hebrews meant by this term. In Hebrews 1:3, the term *hypostasis* clearly has a philosophical sense: Christ is the stamp of the very being (*hypostasis*) of

God. In Hebrews 3:14, the term refers to the initial "conviction" that must be held firm to the end. There, the term also has a philosophical sense: a conviction is something we know to be *real*. So here, in Hebrews 11:1, we should also expect a more philosophical sense for the term. Faith is the *reality* (what we know to be true) of things hoped for.

The thrust of this definition of faith is temporal. That is, it focuses on time. Hebrews stresses looking toward the future. We are to press forward, straining toward a destination we have not yet reached. We are on the way to the Promised Land; we are not yet there. We go forward in hope. Faith gives reality to this hope. It is not blind hope or blind faith. It is based on something that happened (Jesus' death), and it looks toward something that will happen (God's culmination of creation). Sharing in the life of Christ by living faithfully gives our hope substance. Faith is the reality of hope.

"Faith is the *proof* of things unseen." In this part of the definition, the focus is spatial. That is, the author looks not to time and the future but to heaven and what is really real. The term rendered here "proof" is *elengchos*. Many translations render it "conviction," but "confirmation" would be more in keeping with the way this term is used in Greek literature as a whole. It refers to something that has been tested and proven true; it has been confirmed. It is not only what we believe or even know to be true; it is something verified beyond what we believe or think we know.

Faith is the verification or confirmation of something we cannot see. We cannot see the heavenly world. We cannot see into the true heavenly sanctuary. We cannot behold the holy presence of God. But, again, we do see Jesus (2:9). In Hebrews 12:2, we will be urged to keep our eyes on Jesus as we run the race of faith. The faithfulness of Jesus the pilgrim-son who fulfilled his mission and now serves as the pilgrim-priest is our proof that our pilgrimage is not in vain. Despite all the evidence to the contrary in this visible world, by our own faith and faithfulness we see more. Faith is the proof of things unseen.

This kind of faith was real and confirming for the faithful saints of the past (11:2). Such ancient (literally, "elders") pilgrims were both confirmed "in their faith" and confirmed as "truly faithful." What they had faith in was verified, and they were proven to be faithful. Their faithfulness is catalogued throughout the rest of chapter 11, giving us a virtual "Hall of Fame" of the faithful.

The list of those who lived by faith begins with the act of creation (11:3). Our very understanding of how the cosmos came to be is rooted in faith that God creates what is seen out of what is not seen. The creation attests to the creative power of a God who is good, and it points forward toward that destination for which creation was intended.

The following résumé of those who lived by faith is divided into several groups: (1) those who lived before the Flood; (2) Abraham, the great model of faith; (3) Abraham and his descendants; (4) Moses and the Exodus generation; and (5) those who lived after Israel's establishment in the Promised Land. Many themes and images used earlier in Hebrews reappear in these examples of faith, but the overall theme is that these saints of faith looked forward to that which was to come, trusting in God to fulfill the promise.

Those Who Lived before the Flood (11:4-7)

Three antediluvian Old Testament characters are pointed to as examples of faith: Abel, Enoch, and Noah. Each exhibited at least one quality of faith discussed elsewhere in Hebrews.

Abel (11:4) offered a better sacrifice than did Cain. Exactly why it was better is not made clear in Genesis or Hebrews. God's preference of Abel's sacrifice led Cain to murder his brother. Abel died, but "through his faith" he still speaks. How does Abel still speak? Later, Hebrews 12:24 refers to Jesus' sprinkled blood that speaks more graciously than Abel's blood. This verse alludes to Genesis 4:10 wherein God said that Abel's blood cried out from the ground into which it was spilled. Jewish literature sometimes likened Abel's crying blood to that of the martyr calling out to God for vindication. Even dead, Abel still voices his faith in the righteousness of God.

Enoch (11:5-6) appears as one who by faith entered into the presence of God. This connects with the exhortation in 10:22 where readers are urged to draw near with a true heart in full assurance of faith. Hebrews 11:6 reminds us that one cannot draw near to God except in faith. Details about Enoch are drawn from Genesis and later Jewish legends.

Noah (11:7) received a message from God about the coming flood. He trusted in God's message about something unseen and acted faithfully on that message in building the ark. As a result, he joined the line of those inheriting the promised righteousness. The motif of inheritance, alluded to in earlier sections, is referred to repeatedly in chapter 11.

Abraham, the Great Model of Faith (11:8-16)

Abraham receives special attention, which is understandable in light of his exemplary role in the biblical tradition as a model of human faithfulness. By faith, Abraham obeyed God's call to go to an unseen land, dwelled in that land as a pilgrim, and, with Sarah, conceived the child of promise. Abraham and his descendants received the same promise of inheritance made to others. He believed the promise and looked forward to that yet unseen city to be made by God.

The example of Abraham includes a general statement about all those who died in faith (11:13-16). They lived as pilgrims on the earth, strangers and exiles, not receiving their promised inheritance but trusting that it would come. They desired something better than that which they experienced. Their faith is assured of vindication.

Abraham and His Descendants (11:17-22)

The story of Abraham continues. The central episode in Abraham's long pilgrimage of faith was the near sacrifice of Isaac (Gen 22:1-14). Abraham acted in faith, even to the point of willingly offering up the child of promise, Isaac, because he trusted in God's power to resurrect from the dead. Isaac and Jacob, in turn, acted in faith by pronouncing blessings that would find realization only in the future. Joseph, likewise, upon his death, pointed his descendants toward the future and God's act of deliverance in the Exodus.

Moses and the Exodus Generation (11:23-31)

Faith permeates the author's summary of Moses' story. His parents resisted fear of the pharaoh's edict in hiding their son. Moses willingly embraced suffering as one of God's people rather than enjoy the safety and luxury of another way of life. He went into exile in faith and became the instrument of God's deliverance of the enslaved Hebrews through the plagues that culminated in the passing over of the "Destroyer of the firstborn."

Those who were a part of the Exodus story exhibited the same faith as Moses (11:29-31). The people crossed the parted sea and encircled the walls of Jericho. Rahab, too, acted in faith in befriending the Hebrew spies. All these of the Exodus exhibited the courageous faith that is required of pilgrims.

Those Who Lived in the Promised Land (11:32-40)

Six persons from the early history of Israel in the land of promise are named (Gideon, Barak, Samson, Jephthah, David, and Samuel). Then a retinue of faithful acts is recounted that stems from events in the stories about these six men and from other stories both in and outside the Old Testament. Behind the faithful acts named lie traditions about unnamed prophets, women, and martyrs well known to Hebrews' first readers. Some of the acts described may be tentatively connected to certain traditions, especially those that told of events during the so-called Maccabean period of Jewish history. Jewish writings about brave men and women who chose death rather than compromise their faith had special appeal to Christians who encountered similar threats.

Our author, however, is not concerned that the readers know particular persons and times, but rather that they understand that people of faith in all times and places have both triumphed and suffered through faith. For all of the saints of faith, both confirmed in and confirmed by their faith, the object of their hopes lay in the future (11:39). Their hopes, held by faith, were unrealized. Our author's point in stressing this is to direct the whole community of faith, past and present, toward the future. All the faithful live as a community of pilgrims in their own times. The faithful of all times exist as a community of pilgrims that shall inherit the promise together (11:40).

REACHING TOWARD THE FUTURE
(12:1-29)

The final and grandest exhortation to the pilgrimage of faith begins in Hebrews 12:1. It builds on the long list of the faithful given in chapter 11: "Therefore, since we are surrounded by so great a cloud of witnesses." Athletic imagery returns here both in the call to "run the race" and in the references to "witnesses." The word for "witness" is *martys*. It later came to mean one who died for the faith. At this stage in Christian history, it did not yet carry that meaning. Here it probably has two meanings, one athletic and the other more legal. A *martys* could be anyone one who witnessed an event, even as a "spectator" in a stadium. That imagery is present here, but there is more. In a legal setting, a *martys* gave testimony to the facts of a case. Witnesses attested to the truth of what was said. Both at the beginning (11:2) and at the end of the list of the faithful (11:39) those described were said to have been "attested" (based on another form of the word *martys*). Those who make up the great cloud of witnesses, those who occupy the stadium upon whose track the readers must now run, have themselves run the race and have been proven faithful.

Thus, the call comes to pilgrims in the present to run the race. Running faithfully involves at least three things. (1) They must lay aside the weights and sins that would hold them back. Foremost among these would be the fear and sluggishness that have concerned our author throughout. (2) They must run with perseverance, which suggests that the race is more of a marathon than a dash. (3) Most importantly, they must run with their eyes on Jesus.

This final requirement for running places Jesus among the faithful as the supreme paradigm of faith. In fact, he is the "pioneer and perfecter" of faith (12:2). The first title for Jesus here, pioneer (*archēgos*), was used earlier in 2:10 to speak of Jesus as the first of many who would complete the course. The same idea was present in 6:10 when the term forerunner (*prodromos*) was used of Jesus as the one who has preceded his people into the inner sanctuary. But here, combined with the term perfecter (*teleiōtes*), the term *archēgos* carries also the idea that Jesus is somehow the *initiator* of faith just as he is the *finisher* of faith. Thus, he is more than simply the leader; he is the one who makes faith possible, from beginning to end. His life of faithfulness unto death, which led to his exaltation, has opened the way of faith for others.

This Jesus, upon whom faithful runners should gaze, must be seen as the one who willingly endured the cross, despised its shame, and is now enthroned (12:2). His willingness to suffer is now itself a source of inspiration: "Consider him who submitted to such hostility from sinners," so that you will not "lose heart or grow weary" (12:3). All the great saints of faith listed in chapter 11 now fade into the background as the spotlight falls on the supreme example of faithfulness—Jesus. In light of his example, how can the faithful not run tirelessly!

In Hebrews 12:4, the author turns to a different motive for not growing weary. The readers are reminded that none of them has yet paid the price of life itself in their struggles. They should view the sufferings they have encountered as discipline. Proverbs 3:11-12, which includes the statement, "The Lord disciplines those He loves," is cited in support of this point. The fact that they have suffered means that God considers them to be worthy as children (12:7). If God did not love them as children, they would not experience the discipline of suffering.

The author's tactic here assumes a context in which severe discipline, probably even physical, was understood to be a normal responsibility of parenthood. In that context, children were expected to show respect to the disciplining parent. If the readers understood that discipline from a parent should be met with respect, then surely they could see that God's disciplining of them through suffering should be accepted as a part of the good intention of God (12:10). It is part of the process of training for righteousness (12:11).

The two incentives, the example of Jesus who triumphed through suffering and the understanding of suffering as discipline, now become the basis for an exhortation to show a courageous faith (12:12). Drooping hands and weak knees must be strengthened so that they can run straight. As a community ("with everyone"), they are to pursue peace and holiness (12:14).

This exhortation contains a warning that draws from two Old Testament images. One is the "root of bitterness" referred to in Deuteronomy 29:18. In Deuteronomy, the concern was idolatry and departure from the covenant community. Hebrews warns against letting such an attitude infect and defile the new covenant community. The second image is that of Esau from Genesis 25:29-34. Esau sold his birthright for a bowl of porridge because he was "immoral and irreligious" (12:16). Though he later regretted losing his inheritance, he was given no second chance (12:17). The danger of presuming that they will have another opportunity should they fail to be faithful is made clear to the readers.

The warning continues by once again contrasting what they would be giving up with what was offered through the old covenant (12:18-24). The revelation of God to Moses on Mount Sinai, with all of its accompanying terror, is vividly described. The sight was so overwhelming that the people could not touch the holy mountain, and even Moses confessed his fear (12:20-21). Something even grander than the Sinai revelation lies before the readers. They can approach the true mount of revelation, Mount Zion, the heavenly city of Jerusalem, made accessible to them by the sprinkled blood of Jesus (12:22-24).

The warning climaxes in a contrast of the voice that spoke from Mount Sinai with the voice that now speaks to them from heaven (12:25-29). Those who rejected God's call from Sinai suffered rejection by God. Those who now reject God's more compelling call cannot expect a better fate. The voice from Sinai shook the earth and sifted the faithful from the faithless. The voice from heaven sifts all that can be shaken away from that which cannot, God's unshakable kingdom (12:28). Those to whom God has given this kingdom must respond in faithful worship, filled with reverence and awe. The same awesome call that began this final movement is sounded here near the end in full volume.

CARING FOR ONE ANOTHER ON THE WAY
(13:1-19)

The climax of the book's argument has been reached with the powerful description of the heavenly dwelling for God's faithful ones. But, the faithful ones are not there yet. They must live as pilgrims in this world. They must consider now how to stir one another up to show love and do good works, as they were urged to do in the opening exhortation (10:24). The author now tries to spell out what that involves in greater detail. The final chapter contains two clusters of admonitions to faithful living: verses 1-6 and verses 7-19.

The first cluster begins with the imperative, "Let brotherly love (*philadelphia*) abide!" To this general command are added two specific admonitions: show hospitality (13:2) and remember those in prison (13:3). The call to show hospitality is buttressed with an allusion to "entertaining angels unaware." The allusion would have brought to mind various biblical stories such as Abraham and Sarah's encounter with messengers from God in Genesis 18, but the idea of unidentified angelic visitors was a common motif in Greco-Roman stories, too. Our author has earlier commended the readers for their support of prisoners (10:34).

These instructions about expressing love to fellow believers are followed by admonitions that focus on two issues of personal morality: sexual purity in marriage (13:4) and material goods (13:5). Avoiding the entrapment of worldly possessions is supported with a reference to Psalm 118:6 that assures the readers of God's help (13:6). This admonition also connects with a previous commendation of their willingness to suffer the loss of earthly goods (10:34).

The second cluster (13:7-19) begins and ends with instructions about leaders. The first word about leaders urges the readers to imitate those who proclaimed to them the word of God (13:7). Just as they were called to focus on Jesus in 12:2-3, they are called to look to those who have faithfully followed him. "Consider the outcome of their life" possibly suggests that they had died for the faith. Their faithfulness is to be imitated.

Though the faithful leaders may have passed from the scene, the faithful model of Jesus Christ remains: "He is the same yesterday and today and forever" (13:8). Thus, believers must stand firm and not be led astray by strange teachings. The heart is to be strengthened by grace, not by foods (13:9). The reference to foods is odd. It probably serves to continue the contrast between the ways of the old covenant that focused on externals and the way of the new covenant that deals with the inner being. This reading is supported by the reference one final time to the old cultic practice of animal sacrifice "outside the camp" (13:11). Those who depend on such sacrifices cannot partake of the true sacrifice (13:10).

What believers can do is follow after Jesus, the true sacrifice, who was also offered "*outside* the camp" (13:12-13). The reference to Jesus' death outside the camp may carry an allusion to his crucifixion outside the city walls of Jerusalem. It may also carry an appeal to come out from the protective umbrella of Judaism, represented here in Hebrews consistently in the language of the tabernacle and wilderness wandering. Most probably, however, the phrase "outside the camp" simply reemphasizes the persistent theme of Hebrews that believers must be faithful pilgrims daring to live as nomads without a lasting earthly home. This assumption finds support in the reminder that pilgrims seek a city that is yet to come (13:14). Such a life of pilgrimage must be ongoing; it is how Christians "continually offer up a sacrifice of praise to God" (13:15). The admonition to "bear the abuse" of Christ also reminds us again of his sacrificial death. Though his death was "once for all," pilgrims too must willingly travel the road that leads through death to the glory beyond.

The cluster of instructions closes with a reference to current leaders, including the author (13:17-19). Such leaders are entrusted with caring for the souls of their followers, much as shepherds care for their sheep. They are accountable to God for their leadership. So is our author, and he is certain that in this matter his conscience is pure. Still, he requests their prayers in his behalf, knowing that his own pilgrimage is intimately tied to that of his readers. Faithful pilgrimage involves a community of caring.

CLOSE: THE GOD OF PILGRIMS
(13:20-25)

BENEDICTION
(13:20-21)

The body of the long sermon that is Hebrews closes with a beautiful benediction. God is the "god of peace," a most appropriate way to describe God given the stress on living peacefully in the preceding section. God "brought Jesus again from the dead." This is more than a reference to the resurrection, which is central to all New Testament writings. Our author does not use the usual word for "resurrection" or "raising up" here. Instead, he uses a term that means to "bring up." For Hebrews, Christ's resurrection is more than a return to the living; it is an exaltation. Jesus has been led up to the heavenly presence of God.

Now, Jesus is our "leader." This is conveyed through the image of Jesus as the "great shepherd of the sheep" (13:20). Other leaders care for those entrusted to them (13:17). Even Moses is alluded to as a "shepherd of the sheep" in Isaiah 63:11. But, Jesus is the "great" shepherd, made so by God through his blood of the eternal covenant. The same God who "perfected" Jesus in his obedient suffering now stands ready to equip the faithful with "everything good" through Jesus Christ so that they may fulfill their calling (13:21). To this God, glory belongs forever.

EPISTOLARY ENDING
(13:22-25)

The close of the book is the only true epistolary feature in it. The author "exhorts" the readers to "bear with" his word of "exhortation" (13:22). For our author to call his work a "brief" word is ironic.

The reference to Timothy (13:23) has been read by many interpreters as a clue that Paul was the author. Others have seen the reference as a rather modest effort by the actual author to connect the writing to Paul. Still, others see it as a later addition by someone other than the author. The epistolary ending has probably been added to what was otherwise a complete work, but by our author (not Paul) rather than someone else later. Most likely, the reference to Timothy is genuine to the writing and reflects the author's concern to inform the readers about Timothy's condition. It also connects with his own plans to travel to see them, with Timothy. Letters typically contained such travel information near the end.

The greetings are also standard for a letter's close (13:24). His greetings are extended to the whole community, leaders and other saints. The inclusion of greetings from "the Italians" is puzzling. It could mean that the work was written in and sent from Rome. Or, it could refer to a group of former residents of Rome who are present with the author elsewhere. Still, calling them "Italians" rather than "Romans" is unusual.

The final word is a word of grace (13:25). Such a "grace benediction" is standard for letters, but in light of all that our author has written about God's great gift of salvation through Jesus, it is especially appropriate here. The faithful who respond to God's call to pilgrimage can trust that grace will guide their journey.

FOR FURTHER READING

Attridge, Harold W. *Hebrews.* Hermeneia. Philadelphia: Fortress Press, 1989.

Bruce, F. F. *The Epistle to the Hebrews.* The New International Commentary on the New Testament. Grand Rapids: Wm. B. Eerdmans Publishing Co., 1964.

Isaacs, Marie E. "Hebrews." *Mercer Commentary on the Bible.* Macon GA: Mercer University Press, 1995.

_____. *Reading Hebrews and James: A Literary and Theological Commentary.* Smyth & Helwys Publishing, Co., 2001.

Johnsson, William G. Hebrews. Knox Preaching Guides. Atlanta: John Knox Press, 1980.

Käsemann, Ernst. *The Wandering People of God: An Investigation of the Letter to the Hebrews.* Trans. Roy A. Harrisville and Irving L. Sandberg. Minneapolis: Augsburg Publishing House, 1984.

Lane, William L. *Hebrews* 1–8. Word Biblical Commentary 47a. Waco TX: Word Books, 1991.

_____. *Hebrews* 9–13. Word Biblical Commentary 47b. Waco TX: Word Books, 1991.

Westcott, B. F. *The Epistle to the Hebrews.* 2d ed. New York: The Macmillan Co., 1892.

Chapter 2

James
The Lifestyle of Pilgrims

Introduction

THE SIGNIFICANCE OF JAMES

Between the setting out on pilgrimage and the safe arrival in the desired country lies the dangerous journey. Most often the journey is long and complex. Hearing the call to pilgrimage and having a view of the final destination are vital for the pilgrim, but so is having a sense of the twists and turns in the road. Pilgrims need guidance along the way.

James joins with other books standing in the canon of New Testament Scriptures between Hebrews and Revelation that provide guidance for the pilgrim's journey. No other book in this section, and perhaps none in the entire New Testament, gives as much specific guidance about so many aspects of the lifestyle pilgrims are called to follow.

THE EPISTLE OF STRAW

The book of James has unfortunately long lived under the shadow of Martin Luther's now famous assessment of it. In his preface to his German translation of the New Testament, the herald of the Protestant Reformation declared of James: "Therefore, St. James' epistle is really an epistle of straw, compared to these others (the books that he argued 'show you Christ'), for it has nothing of the nature of the gospel about it." He went on to assert that James was deficient because it was flatly against St. Paul and all the rest of Scripture in ascribing justification to works and in its failure to mention the Passion, the Resurrection, or the Spirit of Christ. He concluded that James was written by some Jew who had heard of Christ but who had never encountered him. Among Protestants these perceived deficiencies led to a neglect of James. Though Catholic scholars tended to affirm James in the canon, largely because it buttressed their arguments against Protestants, even some of them had reservations about its authenticity as a letter from the brother of Jesus.

Questions about James, however, did not begin with the Reformation. James appears in none of the lists of Christian scriptures that emerged in the second century, a strong indication that it was not widely known or accepted in the churches. The first certain reference to the book was in the apocryphal *Epistle to the Virgins* from the early third century. The great Alexandrian scholar Origen quoted from James in the third century but acknowledged that it was a disputed book. In the early fourth century Eusebius included James in his list of Christian scriptures but noted that many rejected it. Christians in the East tended to accept it earlier than those in the West where its place in the canon was secured in the fifth century only after Jerome's Latin Vulgate included it.

While most of the writings known as "Catholic Epistles" have received less attention than the Gospels or Paul's letters, James' lack of information about the historical Jesus and its inattention to theological issues have resulted in its special neglect. Nonetheless, scholars have come around to a greater appreciation for James. Some have found it to be an important source for information about how the early church engaged in teaching its members about the Christian life. Johann Gottfried Herder (1884) wrote: "If the Epistle is 'of straw,' then there is within that straw a very hearty, firm, nourishing, as yet uninterpreted and unthrashed, grain." Frank Stagg has argued that Luther simply overlooked the "grain" in James. In 1969 he wrote, "Its theological importance is wanting only if teachings and actions attributed by the Gospels to Jesus are deemed irrelevant to Christian theology."

THE STRENGTH OF JAMES

The importance of James for the New Testament is its dual focus on the practical and the personal dimensions of the Christian life. Students of the New Testament who perceive Christianity primarily as a matter of belief or who prefer to engage in discussions of general, abstract theological ideas find little of interest in James. Those, however, who view actions as at least equally important to belief find much to ponder in James. Those inclined toward specifics rather than generalities also find a friend in James. James engages the question: "How then should we live?" Concrete, relevant answers are given that surely reveal the struggles of pilgrims on the way in a particular time and place, though we cannot be certain when or where that was. Within the context-generated specifics, however, lie a number of abiding principles that offer guidance to Christians of all times and places. James urges pilgrims to reflect on their own situations and to seek ways to live out the gospel amidst the struggles of existence. James helps us transform the grand vision of the call to pilgrimage that leads to the desired destination into tangible steps to take on the way.

THE SETTING OF JAMES

THE BIBLICAL SETTING

James clearly stands in the historical, theological, and literary streams of biblical tradition. When viewed against the background of the major traditions within the Old Testament, James' connections with them become apparent. We can identify those major Old Testament traditions as Law, Prophets, and Wisdom. While elements of these three can be found throughout the Old Testament, certain sections give greater emphasis to specific traditions.

The tradition of Law, or Torah, is paramount in the Pentateuch, the first five books. This tradition focuses on God's revelation in certain events. Foremost among all events is the Exodus. The Exodus event consisted both of God's miraculous deliverance of Israel from slavery in Egypt and God's giving of the Law at Mount Sinai. Both acts signified God's love and purpose for Israel. God's people, redeemed by God's grace, were to live holy lives grounded in the word of God.

The Prophetic tradition, found predominantly in the historical books of Joshua, Judges, 1 and 2 Samuel, and 1 and 2 Kings, and in the books bearing prophets' names (Isaiah, Jeremiah, Ezekiel, and The Twelve Minor Prophets), stressed the role of God's messengers in confronting Israel with God's requirements. Like the Law tradition, the Prophetic tradition was rooted in a sense of covenant. God had established a special relationship with Israel that involved Israel living a special way. The Law tradition emphasized the revelation of this way at Mount Sinai, while the Prophetic tradition focused on the continuing direction of God through prophetic messengers.

Another tradition, Wisdom, can be seen to dominate the third section of the Old Testament, referred to as the Writings in the Hebrew Bible. Job, Ecclesiastes, Proverbs, and many of the Psalms exhibit this tradition. Wisdom stressed reason rather than revelation and tended to focus on the individual rather than on the community as a whole. More philosophical than the other two traditions, Wisdom struggled with issues such as why the righteous suffer (Job) and the purpose of human existence (Ecclesiastes). Much of Wisdom, however, focused on the tangible details of how persons should live day to day (Proverbs). Wisdom could draw from other cultures to define the life to be lived by the wise person, but it also viewed the Law of God as the supreme guide (see especially Psalm 1).

James connects with all these traditions but reflects especially much of the Wisdom tradition. In fact, James resembles Proverbs in its assemblage of various instructions on numerous topics. Like Proverbs, too, James focuses on what one is to do. In defining appropriate action, James follows the Wisdom pattern of drawing from different streams of influence. Yet James also understands, as did Old Testament Wisdom, that the wisdom that comes from above is superior to earthly wisdom (3:17). As did Wisdom, James finds guidance in God's covenant demands, especially in the "Royal Law" (2:8).

When viewed against the background of the rest of the New Testament, James most closely resembles the teaching of Jesus found in the Sermon on the Mount in Matthew's Gospel both in content and in form. Most of the teaching in the Sermon on the Mount and in James can be classified as *paraenesis*. Though the term is used in different ways by different people, it basically refers to teaching that uses general maxims, proverbs, aphorisms, and stock topics. Rather than engaging in a lengthy or complicated analysis or debate of an issue, paraenesis resorts to conventional wisdom as it is expressed in easily remembered sayings. Paraenesis is concerned to influence persons to a particular way of thinking and acting by drawing on traditions that, for the most part, are familiar to both the writer and the readers. Thus, paraenesis rarely includes entirely new teachings, although the particular way traditional material is arranged and articulated may be quite different from its use elsewhere. The *content* of parenetic material is usually general in focus and not related to a particular situation. The *selection* of parenetic units and their arrangement, however, may reveal much information about the specific setting and goal of the writer. While some paraenesis appears in other writings, especially portions of Paul's letters, only James consists entirely of paraenesis.

One particular type of paraenesis found in James is the *topos*. A *topos* was essentially a teaching about a specific topic. The teaching contained a particular ethical instruction, to which were joined supporting reasons and illustrations. James is largely a collection of *topoi* with little or no connections between the different topics. James moves from compact discussions about trials, hearing and doing the word, impartiality, faith and works, the tongue, true wisdom, worldly mindedness, and patience without pulling all these topics into any organized scheme.

In discussing the various topics, James does not appeal to the example of Jesus for guidance. Nor does James quote the words of Jesus, although several of the sayings in James resemble several of Jesus' teachings in the Sermon on the Mount. Nonetheless, more than any other New Testament writer, the author of James follows the example of Jesus as a teacher.

THE HISTORICAL SETTING

What can we detect, then, from the teachings included in James about the circumstances of the author and the first readers? All other New Testament letters at least give us some clues about geographical location, but James mentions only that its intended readers were "the twelve tribes of the dispersion." The term "twelve tribes" obviously has some connection with the heritage of Jews. So does the term "dispersion" (Greek *diaspora*) since Jews living outside the land of Palestine had so been called at least since the time when the Hebrew Scriptures were translated into Greek beginning in the third century B.C. Both because of forced relocation and exile and because of voluntary immigration for economic and even proselytizing purposes the Jews were recognized as a "scattered" people. James' use of diaspora signifies that he perceived his audience as dispersed in some sense. Hence, we can draw no exact clues as to their location.

Calling them the "twelve tribes" connected them further to the Jewish heritage, but we should remember that by the first century the twelve tribes of Israel no longer existed. Jews could still trace their lineage in the tribes of Judah, Levi, and Benjamin, but the other ten tribes had essentially ceased to exist as identifiable entities in the eighth century B.C. The "twelve tribes" had become something of a symbol for Jews, referring to the whole of Israel either in the past or in some future restoration. Christians often used the term symbolically to express their conviction that the Church had become the new, true Israel of God. James may have used the term to remind his Christian readers of their continued connection to the Jewish heritage, a heritage he understood to require righteous living.

The topics James addresses suggest a few knowable aspects of the readers' setting. He briefly mentions trials (1:2-4, 12-16; 2:6), but he does not give details. James 2:6 indicates that some Christians had experienced hardships at the hands of the rich and powerful, and James has much to say about matters of wealth (1:9-11; 2:1-6; 5:1-6). James views the rich very negatively, apparently partly in reaction to certain preferences being granted to them within the congregations to whom he wrote. He addresses divisions within his readership stemming not only from matters of wealth and class status but also from disagreements about true wisdom (1:5-8; 3:13-18) and the relationship of faith and works (2:14-26). Much attention is given to ending the divisive conflicts and disputes that seem to have plagued their ranks (2:19-27; 3:1-12; 4:1-12; 5:9).

What we see, then, is a fractured body of believers, bickering among themselves over issues of status and superior wisdom. Some presume to judge others as to their lack of understanding of matters of faith or their lower stations in life. James argues for righteous living that holds compassion and care for others in the highest regard. Higher social status or claims to higher knowledge sidetrack faithful pilgrims from the primary calling of a holy lifestyle. Without too much imagination, one can see how relevant his words are for the modern church.

Who was James? Tradition identifies the author as the brother of Jesus who, according to the book of Acts and a few other ancient sources, attained a leading role in the Jerusalem church and within the Jewish wing of early Christianity. No other James from antiquity has risen as a viable alternative. The Jewish tone of the book, so despised by Luther, has also supported the connection of this writing with one who was remembered for his Jewish piety. The use of Hellenistic rhetoric, the affirmation of principles characteristic of Hellenistic Judaism (such as worship of God and righteous living), the use of the Greek version of the Hebrew Scriptures, and the lack of concern with those matters that characterized the Jews and Jewish Christians of Palestine (such as circumcision and kosher eating rules) tend to place the book in a context of Hellenistic Jewish Christianity similar to what is known to have existed in places such as Antioch in Syria. The late appearance of this book among the writings widely used in the churches also suggests that it was written at a time when the Jewish roots of the faith were being forgotten as Christians focused on acquiring the status and other privileges of rank afforded them in the Greco-Roman culture. The author was invoking the tradition of the righteous James as a way of calling readers back to holy living. Whoever wrote James knew quite well the challenges confronting faithful pilgrims traveling in a world that offers much that is attractive but inherently counter to the life Christ intended. Again, the continuing relevance is clear.

THE MESSAGE OF JAMES

THE STRUCTURE OF THE BOOK

James resembles a letter only in the opening verse. In this one brief verse we find the identification of the sender, the naming of the addressees, and the typically Greek greeting that one should expect in a letter. Nothing that follows fits the pattern of ancient letters. Instead we have a string of teachings about various topics (*topoi*). No sustained argument guides the discussion of subjects. One could begin reading with any of the topics, and one could stop reading with any one of them. In fact, James itself ends rather abruptly without any formal close.

What we do find is a kaleidoscopic discussion of numerous elements of behavior. Observing the way these elements are grouped together gives us the following arrangement for the book of James.

Prescript (1:1)
Concerning Trials (1:2-18)
    Faith and Wisdom (1:2-8)
    Poverty and Wealth (1:9-11)
    Temptation and Sin (1:12-15)
    God's Good Gifts (1:16-18)
Concerning Hearing and Doing the Word (1:19-27)
    Hearing and Receiving (1:19-21)
    Doers of the Word (1:22-25)
    The Test of Religion (1:26-27)
The Impropriety of Partiality (2:1-13)
    Partiality Incompatible with Faith (2:1-7)
    Partiality Incompatible with Fulfilling the Law (2:8-13)
Faith and Works (2:14-26)
    Statement of the Issue (2:14-17)
    Inseparableness of Faith and Works (2:18-26)
Sayings about the Tongue (3:1-12)
    The Tongue's Power (3:1-5a)
    The Tongue's Uncontrollable Nature (3:5b-8)
    The Tongue's Inconsistent Function (3:9-12)
Sayings about Strife (3:13–4:12)
    True Wisdom: The Solution for Strife (3:13-18)
    Friendship with the World: The Source of Strife (4:1-6)
    Submission to God: The Strategy against Strife (4:7-12)
Sayings about the Worldy-Minded (4:13–5:6)
    The Presumptuous (4:13-17)
    The Prosperous (5:1-6)
Sayings about Christian Conduct (5:7-20)
    Instructions for the Interim (5:7-12)
    Care for Other Pilgrims (5:13-20)

A SYNOPSIS OF THE THEMES

After the brief epistolary opening James begins to give a series of self-contained units of exhortation about a variety of topics. The first of these units concerns trials (1:2-18). James affirms the value of difficult experiences for the process of spiritual maturation. To understand such trials in this positive light, James advises the pilgrim to seek the wisdom of God's perspective, trusting that God will provide. Trusting God is contrasted to trusting in one's other resources, especially wealth, which is fleeting. The faithful should understand that any trials that come are not sent as a temptation from God. God is the source of good gifts, not temptation, which arises from one's own desires.

James then moves to a discussion of hearing and doing the word (1:19-27). The pilgrim must be receptive to this word, rooting out the anger and angry speech that hinder its production of the desired righteousness. Hearing the word must involve acting on it. Hearing without acting is useless, but doing the word brings blessing. The test of true religion can be found in simple, but profound, acts of caring for the needy and caring for one's own spiritual well-being.

The focus then turns to the problem of showing partiality, which was apparently occurring among the readers (2:1-13). James cites the example of favoring the prominent over the poor as a case of evil thinking. He then argues his point by observing that while God has honored the poor with richness in faithfulness, they are bringing dishonor to God by discriminating against the poor. Doing so is a violation of the law of God to love the neighbor. Keeping the law in other points is of no avail if one fails to show mercy to the needy.

James then moves to counter what he considers to be a distorted understanding of the relationship of faith and works (2:14-26). In language that seems to be a direct challenge to certain fundamental ideas of Paul, James asserts that faith without works is dead. James affirms the essential role of doing good deeds for the Christian. Believing the right things is insufficient. Only a faith acted out in righteous living is valid. He even uses the same Old Testament story of Abraham (Gen 16) that Paul had appealed to in arguing for justification by faith to support his contention that faith must be lived out in actions (Rom 4; Gal 3).

The discussion then moves to the problem of holy speech (3:1-12). James acknowledges the power of the human tongue; hence, those who speak must be aware of their awesome responsibility to use the tongue for good. The tongue is depicted as a fire capable of great harm. The stress here is on recognizing the importance of speech and mastering its great potential.

Wisdom again is the focus as James engages in an extended discussion of the causes and cure for strife between Christians (3:13–4:12). In contrast to worldly wisdom, which leads some to boast and thus exalt themselves over others, James advocates seeking the wisdom from above, which leads the faithful to perform works of gentleness and peace. James identifies friendliness with the world and the pursuit of its aims as the source of strife. The cure for such divisive self-exaltation is humility before God. Recognizing the Lord's sovereignty will eliminate the craving to exalt one's self and will enable Christians to refrain from judging others in a worldly way.

James then confronts the "worldly-minded" (4:13–5:6). He exposes the evil of arrogance that leads them to be presumptuous and chastises them for failing to do what they know is right. The rich then receive a severe bashing as James, in a manner reminiscent of such Old Testament prophets as Amos, warns them of the consequences of their abuse of others. Their exploitation is ultimately directed against the Lord.

The final section is a collection of sayings about the conduct of Christians (5:7-20). Above all he urges them to be patient as they await the Lord's return. Hardship should not lead to grumbling against one another. Rather, they should model their behavior after the prophets and others who exhibited patient endurance. Finally, they are called to care for one another. They are to pray in faith for those who suffer, and they are to seek to recover any fellow pilgrims who stray.

Commentary

PRESCRIPT
(1:1)

James begins as a letter with a standard epistolary opening identifying the sender and the recipients and giving a word of greeting. Though tradition has decided that the James named here was the brother of Jesus who became the head of the Jerusalem Christians, we cannot know that for certain. James, or Yacov (Jacob) in Hebrew, was a common name. Several Jameses appear in the New Testament. The technical language and developed literary style of this book almost certainly mean that the Galilean sibling of Jesus would have had to use a scribe to pen the work, if he is to be seen as the author. The Hellenistic features of the book (discussed above), despite its Jewish cast, better fit a non-Palestinian Jewish Christian as the author. The "James" from whom the work comes is simply identified as a "servant of God and the Lord Jesus Christ." The word for servant used here is *doulos*, the same word Paul often used to describe himself and other church workers. The term signifies both ownership (belonging to God and Christ) and humility. It is a fitting title in light of James' appeal to humility throughout the book.

The recipients are identified as the "twelve tribes of the dispersion" (see discussion above). Most likely, this term was used symbolically of the church in recognition of its "dispersed" (and in some sense "wandering") character and to remind the church of its connection to the righteous heritage of Judaism.

The greeting is the typical Greek greeting *chairein* ("greeting"). One might have expected the Hebrew greeting *shalom* or a combination of the two as we find always in Paul's letters.

CONCERNING TRIALS
(1:2-18)

FAITH AND WISDOM
(1:2-8)

The body of the book begins with a discussion of various aspects of trials. The first unit considers the proper perspective on such trials. Trials are to be seen as God's way of purifying the faith of pilgrims. In this, James echoes the similar thinking of two apocryphal books, Sirach and Judith. Sirach 2:1 states, "My son, if you come forward to serve the Lord, prepare yourself for trial." Judith told the elders of her city, "In spite of everything, let us give thanks to the Lord our God, who is putting us to the test as he did our forebears" (8:25). The word translated trial or test is *peirasmos*. The same word could be rendered "temptation," as it should be in James 1:12. But James is careful to distinguish between testing (*peirasmos*) that comes from God and is intended to do good and temptation (*peirasmos*) that does not come from God and is intended to do harm. The good that God intends in such testing is endurance. Endurance, in turn, enables one to attain maturity. Pilgrims mature as they endure.

Probing the question of what meaning could be found in suffering was a common theme of the wisdom tradition. Understanding the true nature of trials requires more than human wisdom, James asserts. Thus, believers should ask God for clearer understanding of their times of testing. They should ask in full faith, trusting in God's goodness. To ask without fully trusting is to be "double-minded," a term that only appears elsewhere in early Christian writings in the second-century work *The Shepherd of Hermas*. There, too, it affirms that "double-minded praying" (we might say "halfhearted") brings no results.

POVERTY AND WEALTH
(1:9-11)

The first of James' attacks on the rich occurs in the next unit. Here James employs a motif that we find elsewhere in Jewish and Christian literature, the idea of the poor as inherently pious. In contrast to theological and social attitudes that attach riches to blessing from God, James shares the view that riches distance one from God. Just as the double-minded person in the previous section is divided in his or her objects of trust, the rich cannot give themselves wholly to faith in God because their trust lies in their wealth. Drawing from Isaiah 40:6-8, James likens the rich to withering flowers. The lowly, according to this world's standards, however, are exalted by God.

TEMPTATION AND SIN
(1:12-15)

James returns to the issue of testing in the next unit. Here he deals with the dark side of the experience, when it is temptation to do evil. His argument is in a sense a theodicy, that is, a justification of the goodness of God in the face of evil. The classic question of theodicy can be framed as, "If God is good and all-powerful, then why does God allow evil to exist?" James explains that evil is rooted in human desire, not in God's will. So, testing (*peirasmos*), when it is temptation (*peirasmos*) to do evil, is not caused by God. Here James echoes again the thought of Sirach (15:11-20) who argued that evil desire was the source of all sin. James also reflects Jewish discussions about the struggle in the human soul between the good impulse and the evil inclination. The Jewish writing known as the *Testament of Joseph* (4:1) stated that the good person who followed the good impulse would receive a crown of glory. James states that the one who endures temptation will receive a crown of life.

GOD'S GOOD GIFTS
(1:16-18)

God is the source of good, not evil. Christians must not be deceived into thinking otherwise, just as they must not be deceived about the true source of temptation. The dual language of good and evil was often symbolized by the contrast between light and darkness (cf. Eph 5:7-10). James calls God the "Father of lights" and uses astronomical terms (variation, shadow, change) that reflect the instability and untrustworthiness of other heavenly "lights" to affirm the faithfulness of God. Changing metaphors, James then asserts that God's activity is aimed at producing good fruit.

CONCERNING HEARING AND DOING THE WORD
(1:19-27)

HEARING AND RECEIVING
(1:19-21)

Having introduced the subject of God's word of truth in verse 18, James turns to discuss hearing and doing the word. The word comes from God; it is implanted, not innate. The words that are innate to humans are often faulty. Hence, James gives three commands: be quick to hear, be slow to speak, be slow to anger. Similar instructions can be found in other wisdom writings (Sirach 5:11, hearing; Prov 29:20, speech; Eccl 7:9, anger). Angry speech is a concern in several places in this book (1:26; 3:5-12; 4:11; 5:9). The human soil in which the word is implanted should be fertile, rid of the wickedness that hinders its growth.

DOERS OF THE WORD
(1:22-25)

Deception also lurks for those who receive the word but do not heed it. Those who hear but do not do the word are likened to those who look in a mirror and quickly forget their reflection. The image could suggest that James means a person who sees his or her reflection but doesn't do any grooming, but more likely the point is the contrast between the fleeting mirror-image and the real person who remains. The idea of the fleeting reflection in the mirror was sometimes used to draw a contrast between what was real and tangible and was only ideal or imaginary. James focuses on the real. Doing is the test of real faith. Hence, the faithful look into the "perfect law of liberty" and do not forget what they see—they live out the faith.

The phrase "perfect law of liberty" calls for some comment. Paul seems to have argued for freedom *from* the law in several of his letters (esp. Romans and Galatians). To see the law as liberating appears to run counter to Paul's view. Indeed, much in James appears to oppose Paul. We should keep in mind that Paul was arguing against those who took pride in certain features of the Mosaic law (esp. circumcision) and used the law as a measuring device for sporting their righteousness. Paul affirmed the good intent of the law and even argued that it found its full expression in the commandment to love one's neighbor (Gal 5:14). James refers to this commandment later as the "royal law" (2:8). Here James is affirming the liberating effect of submitting one's life to the rule of God. In doing so, he reflects a common Jewish perspective that God's law was intended to set one free to live the best life possible, rather than enslave one to a rigid system of petty rules, as many persons today charge the Jewish law of doing. For Jews, the law was God's gift of love. James echoes this appreciation for the law as God's guide.

THE TEST OF RELIGION
(1:26-27)

One's performance is the true test of faith. Being "religious" (today we seem to prefer the word "spiritual") can be exposed as meaningless if the piety is not focused on the tangible. James uses terms for religious (*thrēskos*) and religion (*thrēskeia*) that often referred to acts of worship such as sacrifices. Similarly, he uses language of the sacrificial cult ("pure," "undefiled") to speak of genuine religion. Genuine religion is expressed in tangible acts such as controlling the tongue, caring for widows and orphans, and preserving one's moral integrity. Controlling the tongue gets high priority in James. Tending to the lowly, such as orphans and widows, places James in the good tradition of the Old Testament prophets. Being untarnished by the world's perverted sense of values sets James down firmly in the tradition of Jesus.

THE IMPROPRIETY OF PARTIALITY
(2:1-13)

PARTIALITY INCOMPATIBLE WITH FAITH
(2:1-7)

James now turns to one of his major concerns: showing partiality in the church. The word translated partiality or favoritism literally means "taking face" (*prosōpolāmpsia*). Its origins lie in the custom of kings allowing accepted persons to "lift up their face" in the ruler's presence, hence to be received. The term came to have negative connotations associated with a judge giving unfair, favored treatment. In discussing this matter, James uses a form of the *diatribe*, an ancient type of argument that had the writer or speaker dialoging with an imaginary opponent.

What James says is that partiality is incompatible with faith in Jesus. He uses a stock example to make his case: showing favoritism to the rich. Here he depicts a prominent person dressed in the garb of the upper class visiting an assembly of Christians and receiving preferential treatment over the poorer visitors. One can imagine a modern setting where a celebrity gets front-row accommodations while the smelly wino gets ushered to an obscure seat in the rear. James considers such discriminations to be absolutely counter to the gospel. Furthermore, he finds it hard to understand how Christians could thus honor those rich, powerful persons who have caused so much harm to the faith and to the Christians who go out of their way to please them.

PARTIALITY INCOMPATIBLE WITH FULFILLING THE LAW
(2:8-13)

As James turns to show how partiality is contrary to the law of God, he seems to anticipate a counter argument that might have been made by his imaginary opponent in the diatribe. One might try to defend partiality on the basis of the law in Leviticus 19:15 about not showing partiality to the poor. James counters that true fulfillment of Leviticus 19 requires loving one's neighbor, rich or poor. His reference to the "royal law" should be taken to mean the whole law, not only the commandment to love one's neighbor. His point is that breaking the law by showing partiality in any way makes one guilty of law-breaking. In Galatians 5:3 Paul argued that those who come under the law through circumcision are obligated to keep the whole law. The Stoics also argued that allowing one's vice to remain in one's character was an infringement of the whole demand of virtue. The Stoics also described the virtuous wise person as "kingly." This may be reflected in James' labeling of the law as "royal."

His point here is that showing partiality cannot be construed in any way as compatible with doing the will of God. If God's law is to be liberating, then one must be freed from the social distinctions that determined one's value in ancient society. Mercy, not judgment or discrimination (same root), is to be the dominant quality of those to whom God has shown mercy.

FAITH AND WORKS
(2:14-26)

STATEMENT OF THE ISSUE
(2:14-17)

Probably no section of James has received more attention than this unit in which he discusses the relationship between faith and works. The unit falls into two parts: (1) James introduces the issue and cites an example; (2) James then uses the diatribe as a device to argue his point. At first glance, the passage pits James against Paul, and to a large degree such a reading is inevitable. In Galatians 3, in particular, Paul argues against seeing the works of the law as a means of being justified before God. There he holds out "faith alone" as the way to receiving God's Spirit (Gal 3:2). James asks bluntly: "Can faith save you?" (v. 14). Paul would have shouted, "Yes, faith can save you!" But James argues, "So faith, if it has no works, is dead" (v. 17). This assertion comes right after James points to the case of a person of "faith" speaking comfort to a needy person but doing nothing to address the need.

Are we at an unbridgeable gulf between James and Paul, between Catholicism and Protestantism, between two versions of Christianity? Maybe not. The key to the clear difference in perspective between the two biblical writers is in understanding their terminology. Both use the words "faith" and "works," but both do not mean the same thing by these words. For Paul, faith (*pistis*) was a large, inclusive concept that involved the trusting commitment of one's life to God's salvation in Jesus. Works, for Paul, had a very narrow meaning. Works typically had to do with performing the requirements of the Law of Moses as an essential part of being set right with God. Those who trusted in the works of the law as the way of salvation were not trusting in the work of God in Christ.

James' use of the same words is reversed. For him, faith (*pistis*) is understood in a narrow way to mean "belief," just as it is by many people today. James was convinced that "believing" the right things was of no ultimate value in itself. Works, for James, referred not to the keeping of the Law of Moses in itself, but rather to doing the word, that is, living the righteous life that God intends. Words of belief without acts of righteousness are empty and inconsequential in his view. Orthodoxy (right thinking) takes a backseat to orthopraxy (right doing).

While James may or may not have been taking direct issue with Paul, he does seem to have been opposing those who may have based their arguments on Paul's teachings. He targets the crowd that holds that proper belief is the way to please God. That crowd is still with us devising creeds and confessions of faith that draw circles around the "faithful" and excluding from the ranks of acceptable (or real) Christians those who have different doctrinal views. His flat statement that such understandings of Christianity are "dead" should be taken in full seriousness.

INSEPARABLENESS OF FAITH AND WORKS (2:18-26)

To argue his point, James uses a diatribe that is confusing at first. "But someone will say, 'You have faith and I have works'." This seems to put James on the side of faith (as belief) if he is the "you" being addressed by the imaginary opponent. But this is impossible given the rest of his argument. The "you" is James' opponent, the one who claims to have faith alone. James is the "I," the one who has works. James' response to this opponent is to demand that that person's faith be shown. "Put your faith out here on the table where we can see it," he requests. Of course, faith as belief cannot be seen, only thought and mouthed. But James can show his works as a visible proof of faith.

The central tenet of Jewish belief was that God is one. James argues that assenting to this central doctrinal belief proves nothing since even evil demons can *believe* the right things. Believing something is right and true does not make one a Christian. If so, then the demons are Christians. To show that it is not belief that ultimately matters, James appeals to the example of Abraham in Genesis 16. Paul had used the same story to show that God considered Abraham righteous because of his trust in God (Gal 3:6). James argues that the proof of Abraham's trust in God came in Genesis 22 when he placed Isaac on the altar to be sacrificed. The affirmation of belief in Genesis 16 required the action of Genesis 22 to be meaningful. Abraham's faith was a working faith. Likewise, Rahab the harlot proved her faith through what she did.

Obviously James expresses a higher regard for the works of the law than did Paul. Paul's battle was fought against those who pitted the law against faith (trust) as an alternative means of salvation. James' battle was aimed against those who pitted faith (belief) against action as if salvation were only a matter of the mind. From all the attention Paul gave to proper action in his letters, one can see that the apostle was deeply concerned about righteous living. Faith (as trusting commitment), for Paul, included righteous living. Against those who reduced faith to a matter of belief and with James who argued that faith had to include righteous living, Paul would have said "Amen!"

SAYINGS ABOUT THE TONGUE
(3:1-12)

THE TONGUE'S POWER
(3:1-5A)

In chapter 3 James pinpoints one issue that seems to underlie several of his concerns: the use of the tongue. His opening sentence seems to set the whole discussion in the context of the responsibilities of teachers, but in truth teachers simply serve as a prime example of how the tongue can be misused. Those charged to instruct others carry great liability in what they say, but control of speech is the charge of every Christian. In fact, harnessing speech is seen as the key to keeping the whole body in line.

This observation leads to a discussion of the tongue's power. Two images are used to convey this. The first is that of the bit placed in horses' mouths to control them. The other is that of the rudder used to guide a ship. Both the bit and the rudder are small instruments, yet they dictate the direction of large objects. The Jewish philosophical writer Philo used the images of the helmsman and the charioteer to show how God, through reason, guided the cosmos and to show how humankind, through reason, guided the earth. For Philo, the image of the small thing controlling the greater was used positively, but for James the tongue's tyranny is viewed negatively.

THE TONGUE'S UNCONTROLLABLE NATURE
(3:5B-8)

The philosophical tradition from which Philo drew also compared the lack of control by the helmsman or charioteer (reason) to a raging fire. James introduces this image as he turns to describe the problem of taming the tongue. As it often does, his discussion echoes the words of the apocryphal book of Sirach, which states, "It (the tongue) will not be master over the godly, and they will not be burned in its flame" (28:22). James says the tongue is a raging *fire*. In a poetically structured sentence (v. 6) James portrays the tiny tongue as a cosmos of iniquity in itself, standing among the other members of the body and staining them all, then moving on to infect the whole cycle of life. While every other living thing has been tamed by humans, no one can control the tongue. In stating the seeming impossibility, however, James is insinuating the obligation to try.

THE TONGUE'S INCONSISTENT FUNCTION
(3:9-12)

In pointing out the tongue's potential for good, as well as evil, James again picks up on the language of Sirach (28:12) where it is noted that the breath that inflames a spark and the spit that extinguishes a fire both come from the same mouth. Both blessing and cursing can come from the same tongue. While Judaism allowed certain curses, James argues that only good speech should come forth. The use of nature images to show that only one kind of product (figs, water) should come from a single source (fig tree, spring) is similar to Stoic arguments about the distinct roles of the parts of the natural order. Double talk is as inappropriate as the double-mindedness he criticized earlier (1:7).

SAYINGS ABOUT STRIFE
(3:13–4:12)

TRUE WISDOM: THE SOLUTION FOR STRIFE
(3:13-18)

The reference to "bitter" water in verse 11 provides a linkword to the next section in which James denounces "bitter" envy (v. 14). The concern of this long section is contentious strife. The cure for such strife is given at the start: wisdom from above. Wisdom was understood to be the goal and possession of the sage or teacher. But James is not concerned about abstract, philosophical wisdom. After the fashion of the Jewish wisdom tradition, he is concerned about practical, moral wisdom, the kind that is expressed in righteous behavior.

The opposite of wisdom from above is earthly wisdom manifested in arrogant ambition and contentiousness. James is suspicious of anything that smacks of friendship with the world. Exhibiting the bitter envy and selfish rivalry of the world leads to disorder of community and corruption of character. True wisdom engenders peace and enables the pursuit of righteousness.

FRIENDSHIP WITH THE WORLD: THE SOURCE OF STRIFE (4:1-6)

Continuing his argument, James explains that accommodation to the world's standards stems from the cravings (*ēdonōn*, from which we derive the term *hedonism*) warring within us. These inner cravings bring chaos to the inner self and to the outer world of relationships. James' language and concepts here largely parallel Stoic discussions of the problem of controlling passions. Pleasure-seeking, so often the accepted norm today, as the goal and way of life ultimately makes living the full life intended by God impossible. Jesus said we cannot serve God and mammon. James puts it this way: We're either friends of God or friends of the world. For James, the pursuit of pleasure stands over against God.

SUBMISSION TO GOD: THE STRATEGY AGAINST STRIFE (4:7-12)

The proper tactic to take against strife-generating pleasure-seeking, then, is to submit fully to God. James gives ten short commands, which seem to be based on Proverbs 3:34. Together they constitute an almost irresistible summons to bow down in utter humility before the God who alone can save one from the onslaught of human passion. The words of the prophet Micah also seem to loom large behind James' call to submission: "He has shown you what is good, and what does the Lord require of you but to do justice, and to love kindness, and to walk humbly with your God" (6:8).

The inseparableness of submission to God and humility toward the neighbor is expressed in James' injunction against slander. His earlier concerns about discrimination and verbal abuse come together here. The apocryphal book Wisdom of Solomon (1:11) says that slander destroys the soul and is contrary to the pursuit of God's righteousness. James sees slander as a transgression against the law of God. To reduce the worth of another individual through slander is to discriminate against the law and thus against God. Submission to the supreme judgeship of God frees one from assuming the self-defeating burden of judging others.

SAYINGS ABOUT THE WORLDY-MINDED
(4:13–5:6)

THE PRESUMPTUOUS
(4:13-17)

Having characterized the world as being over against God, James now moves to criticize two particular types of people who exhibit the values of the world: the arrogant and the wealthy. Both groups, which were not mutually exclusive and in James' opinion probably overlapped considerably, are addressed in a style similar to the prophetic indictments of the Old Testament. Both units begin with the imperative "come now" (or "now listen").

The first group consists of the arrogant who presume to know the future. Since they presume to be in control of their lives and affairs, they have every reason to trust that tomorrow will bring more opportunity for conducting business. Their attitude brings to mind the parable of Jesus in Luke's Gospel (12:16-22) about the rich man who assumed that his good business would continue indefinitely and who suddenly died leaving his riches.

The focus of the section is on the uncertainty of life from the human perspective. Life is but a vapor that soon passes. The fault is not in planning for the future but in ignoring the God who holds the future. Thus, James admonishes the arrogant to acknowledge the Lord's sovereignty: "If the Lord wills . . .". The phrase, "If the Lord wills," is actually found quite often in ancient expressions of pagan piety, both genuine and superficial. It resembles the commonly heard phrase "If it's meant to be . . ." voiced by Christians and non-Christians today. In James' usage, however, the phrase becomes a humble recognition that God is the lord of life. Having warned his readers of what is right in this regard, James asserts that failure to live in the light of God is sin.

THE PROSPEROUS
(5:1-6)

The rich receive their harshest condemnation from James in this section. For him, being rich and being wicked are practically the same. His list of calamities awaiting the rich resembles the one in 1 Enoch 97. There, too, the warnings given are not calls to repentance but announcements of what is seen as an inevitable doom. James, in fact, speaks of these disasters as if they have already happened. Their riches have already rotted the wealthy and have, in turn, begun to rot themselves. The rusting of the gold and silver may suggest that instead of giving them as alms to the poor, the coins of the rich have sat idly by accumulating their own erosion. More likely, though, James is depicting the aftermath of the death of the wicked-rich; their coins survive as deteriorating monuments to their evil.

The rich receive special criticism for exploiting their workers, a practice forbidden by Deuteronomy 24 and Leviticus 19. Sirach 34:22 likens withholding pay to the murder of laborers. While the rich are synonymous with evil, the poor seem to be synonymous with right-eousness (v. 6). The exploitation of the righteous by the rich, which has lined their pockets and padded their bank accounts, has also been fattening the wealthy for their own destruction. Amos' "cows of Bashan" (4:1) image comes to mind. In similar fashion, the rich targets of James' vendetta are being prepared for the slaughter.

SAYINGS ABOUT CHRISTIAN CONDUCT
(5:7-20)

INSTRUCTIONS FOR THE INTERIM
(5:7-12)

James now turns away from his criticism of the worldly-minded to give a series of unconnected instructions to those pursuing the godly life. The whole section is set in an eschatological context; he reminds his readers that they live in anticipation of the coming of the Lord. They are pilgrims on the journey that will one day be finished. He wants to give them instructions for the interim.

To encourage patience, James draws an analogy from agriculture. The early and late rains mentioned refer to the first rains of the rainy season coming in late October signaling the time for sowing and the later rains coming in April boosting the crops toward maturity. The farmer waits for both and sows and reaps accordingly. If the farmer can wait with patience for the rains, the pilgrim can wait for the Lord's return, trusting that any delay is according to God's good intentions.

In the interim they should refrain from grumbling (actually, "groaning") against each other, which is the opposite of patience. As encouragement James points to the prophets as models of endurance. That he mentions Job in particular seems odd in two ways. First, Job is not usually considered to be among the prophets, but we should note that often all Old Testament characters of merit could be called prophets. Secondly, a careful reading of Job reveals that he was hardly patient in the usual sense of the word. He complained loudly and often. Job is not commended here for his patience (*makrothymia*) but rather for his endurance (*hypomonē*) evident in his refusal to denounce God despite his hardships.

Even more important than not grumbling is not swearing (v. 12). Jesus issued a similar prohibition against swearing oaths in Matthew

5:24-27. In both Matthew and James the issue is not "cussing" but supporting one's word with some oath that verifies its truth. Such oaths could be elaborate and technically contrived to allow loopholes. Simple speech expressing the truth is preferred.

CARE FOR OTHER PILGRIMS
(5:13-20)

Finally, James turns to the matter of pilgrims caring for one another on the way. The praying and the anointing with oil called for here above all emphasize the communal nature of pilgrim life. Sickness is not to be treated as a private affair with the sick confined to their solitude perhaps to ponder what they had done to bring on their affliction. The sick are to be embraced by the community of faith, and the leaders of prayer are to share the pain of their afflicted fellow travelers.

The scene James describes, with elders being called in and oil being applied, gives us a typical picture of Jewish, and early Christian, village life. Jews and others used oil as a common medicinal tool, sometimes with therapeutic value and sometimes not. It might be paralleled today by giving a fever patient aspirin and offering a prayer. The prayer, not the oil (or aspirin), is the focus here. James believes in the efficacy of prayer, especially the prayer of faith and especially the faithful prayers of the righteous. He recognized what we also know, that some persons have developed the discipline of prayer more than have others. He mentions the prophet Elijah who prayed for drought for three and a half years and then for rain. Since the story about Elijah in 1 Kings 17 does not say he prayed for drought, James seems to be drawing here on later rabbinic tradition that attributed the drought itself to Elijah. Jewish tradition practically elevated Elijah to superhuman status, but James stresses that he was a "human being like ourselves."

James' final instruction concerns those who might stray from the truth. His statement that the person who brings the wanderer back to the fold will "save the sinner's soul from death and will cover a multitude of sins" is somewhat troubling for Protestants. The death the sinner is saved from could be ultimate destruction or it could mean the life expected for the wanderer living with the ravages of sin. Judaism had developed the idea that righteous deeds stored up a treasury of forgiveness in heaven. Whether the sins covered were those of the wanderer, those of the restorer, or simply forgiveness of sin in general is not clear. The clear concern, however, is that Christians assume responsibility for helping and restoring one another on the way. Given the numerous pitfalls James has described in this book, pilgrims can be thankful that they are not called to travel alone but in the company of caring fellow travelers.

FOR FURTHER READING

Culpepper, R. Alan. "James." *Mercer Commentary on the Bible.* Macon GA: Mercer University Press, 1995.

Dibelius, Martin and Heinrich Greeven. *James.* Hermeneia. Trans. M. A. Williams. Philadelphia: Fortress Press, 1976.

Isaacs, Marie. *Reading Hebrews and James: A Literary and Theological Commentary.* Smyth & Helwys Publishing, Co., 2001.

Laws, Sophie. *The Epistle of James.* New York: Harper & Row, 1980.

Martin, Ralph P. *James.* Word Biblical Commentary 48. Waco TX: Word Books, 1988.

Maynard-Reid, P. U. *Poverty and Wealth in James.* Maryknoll NY: Orbis Books, 1987.

Perkins, Pheme. *First and Second Peter, James, and Jude.* Interpretation. Louisville KY: John Knox Press, 1995.

Ropes, J. H. *A Critical and Exegetical Commentary on the Epistle of St. James.* International Critical Commentary. Edinburgh: T. & T. Clark, 1916.

Songer, Harold S. "James." *Broadman Bible Commentary.* Nashville: Broadman Press, 1972.

Chapter 3

1 Peter
The Trials of Pilgrims

Introduction

THE ORIGIN OF 1 PETER

Among the New Testament letters known as the "Catholic Epistles," 1 Peter has regularly held priority in terms of the attention it has received. Several features of the letter account for this. First of all, 1 Peter addresses the matter of Christians under trial, and both the real and perceived threat of persecution for the early church made this letter especially relevant. The ongoing experience of trials for Christians of many times and places has also given 1 Peter a ready audience throughout the ages.

A second reason for 1 Peter's prominence among the lesser attended to Catholic Epistles lies in its portrayal of Christ as one who suffered innocently for doing righteousness. His example stands as a summons for the church to do the same as it faces challenges of various stripes from an often hostile world.

A third reason is its glowing imagery about the church. Some of the most memorable and hopeful visions of the church found anywhere in the New Testament are in 1 Peter 2.

Another reason for its relative popularity, frankly, has been its association with the apostle Peter. Recognized as the chief among the apostles since the early days of the church, Peter's accepted authorship of the letter has enhanced its reception. Understandably, then, questions about that traditional view of authorship have not always been appreciated. Nonetheless, as we consider the origins of 1 Peter, we must address those questions.

AUTHORSHIP

Whenever and wherever 1 Peter was cited in early Christian writings, its Petrine authorship was accepted without question. The first doubts about Peter's having written the letter, though, arose because of observations about the literary style. 1 Peter is written in fluent Greek and uses vocabulary and rhetorical devices that one would not expect from a Galilean fisherman. The Greek is some of the finest in the New Testament in terms of its command of the language. Even when quoting Old Testament Scriptures, the author always cites the Greek version, rather than translate from the Hebrew as one might expect from Peter. The reference to Silvanus in 5:12 has been taken as a clue that he scribed the letter for Peter, and thus the unexpected polished Greek is thought to be explained. But the mention of Silvanus only indicates that he was the carrier of the letter, not its secretary. Furthermore, the style is so removed from what one would expect from Peter that we would have to credit Silvanus, or any scribe, with much of the thought in the letter as well.

More telling than style, though, is the fact that 1 Peter resembles so much found in Paul's letters. Many Pauline concepts and phrases are contained in 1 Peter so as to indicate some awareness of the Pauline tradition and perhaps even of a collection of Paul's letters. One wonders why the foremost apostle would have to depend so heavily on another apostle who was sometimes viewed as his chief rival. Also, one wonders why the "Apostle to the Jews" (Gal 2:7) would have written to gentiles, as the author clearly did in 1 Peter.

Furthermore, one might expect from the hand of Peter the kinds of personal references to his experience as a disciple of Jesus that we see in Peter's speeches in Acts. One might also expect some references to Jesus' teachings. Nothing about Jesus in the letter indicates that the author knew him before his resurrection. What the letter does say about Jesus is similar to what we find in common Christian tradition.

Most telling of all against the traditional view of authorship, however, is the apparent purpose of the letter. The readers appear to have experienced, or were facing the real prospect of, some kind of persecution. While persecution of Christians did occur during the reign of Nero (in fact, Peter is said to have been one of the victims), these were short-term and limited to Rome. 1 Peter is addressed to Christians in northern Asia Minor, a place where the kind of persecution envisioned cannot be firmly dated before decades after the traditional time for Peter's death.

Add to these problems coming from the style and content of the letter itself the external evidence of early Christian writers who knew and used the letter. The earliest direct witness is Irenaeus from the fourth quarter of the second century. Tertullian and Clement of Alexandria also show knowledge of 1 Peter near the end of the second century. Possible allusions to 1 Peter exist in the earlier writing by Polycarp (ca. A.D. 125), but the connections alleged to be found in 1 Clement (written from Rome ca. A.D. 96) are too vague to be convincing. Importantly, Ignatius of Antioch, who traveled through some of the areas mentioned in 1 Peter on his way to Rome around A.D. 105 and wrote several letters to churches nearby, did not seem to know anything about 1 Peter. Since Ignatius was bishop of the church that tradition said had been founded by Peter, one might expect him to have referred to 1 Peter if he had known about it, especially since it deals with many of the same issues he addressed in his letters.

The conclusion drawn here from the internal and external evidence is that 1 Peter probably came sometime after the death of Peter, maybe in the late first or early second century, and that it was written by someone who wanted to draw a strong connection between the letter's message and the apostolic tradition personified by Peter. Such writings in the name of revered leaders were not uncommon and were, in general, not viewed as fraudulent but as respectful efforts to speak as a true representative of the named author. In fact, it has been argued that the letter was penned by someone who could be considered a member of the "Petrine school" within the early church.

SETTING

We cannot know for certain who wrote 1 Peter, nor can we state definitely the circumstances in which it was written. We can, however, draw several probable conclusions about the kind of setting to which it was addressed.

The prescript of the letter states that it was intended for people living in the Asia Minor areas of Pontus, Galatia, Cappadocia, Asia, and Bithynia. These regions made up the bulk of Asia Minor, covering all but the southern coast. 1 Peter calls the addressees "exiles of the dispersion," a label with significant Jewish connotations. As we noted in the previous chapter on James, however, such a label did not mean the readers had to be Jewish Christians. In fact, other indicators in the letter clearly show that the readers were Gentiles. That they were called "exiles" (Greek *parepidēmoi*) is significant. In 2:11 they are called exiles and "aliens" (Greek *paroikoi*). The terms normally referred to resident aliens, that is, people living outside their homeland. Most likely, the author uses these terms symbolically, not politically. They were pilgrims, residing in the various Roman provinces of Asia Minor but not fully as citizens of this world. They were citizens of another community, the chosen people of God (2:9), a holy nation cast among the unholy peoples of this world.

What we can know about people living in these regions in the last decade of the first century and first two decades of the second is revealing. For the most part, prosperity and peace reigned. The Roman empire was entering into its "Golden Age" of the second century, and the cities of Asia Minor were experiencing tremendous growth. While some of 1 Peter's readers were apparently drawn from the lower classes, others seem to have come from more affluent ranks. Their identity as "Christians," however, resulted in certain problems for enjoying the full privileges available within their different societies. As members of an increasingly suspect "cult," Christians in these regions found themselves faced with the challenge of accommodation to the prevailing cultural norms or increased isolation in order to preserve their distinctive values.

The focal point of the various problems for the church was the imperial cult. While Romans tended to be tolerant of non-Roman religions, the official cult of the goddess Roma and her earthly representative, the emperor, gave the Romans a powerful tool for holding the empire together ideologically. A divinely-decreed hierarchy headed by the emperor was thought to guarantee the proper order of things. Disloyalty to this system was considered dangerous for the well-being of society in general and the enjoyment of divine favor in local areas in particular. As we shall see in the chapter on Revelation, Asia Minor was a place where local leadership aggressively pursued the benefits of demonstrating imperial loyalty through promotion of the imperial cult.

Though the actual evidence is ambiguous, Christian resistance to acknowledging the deity of the emperor probably led to some localized persecution during the reign of Domitian (81–96). We can be more certain about local persecution in the reign of Trajan (97–117) because we have correspondence between that emperor and his legate sent to Bithynia to correct the administrative disorder that developed there. The legate, Pliny the Younger, encountered a large number of Christians, so many that the official pagan religious sites and festivals had suffered neglect. Though Pliny knew that Christians had been brought to trial for their disloyalty there in earlier times, he had not dealt with the problem before and needed advice. His correspondence shows that many Christians had been persuaded to give up their dangerous affiliation with this new cult and had returned to full participation in paganism. But some were obstinate and had to be punished, more for their stubbornness and apparent disrespect toward Rome than for their devotion to Christ.

1 Peter speaks to the kind of situation that would have existed in Asia Minor from 90–120. Christians might encounter persecution if their behavior was judged to be harmful to the state. 1 Peter advises Christians to be good citizens and obey the authorities without compromising their loyalty to Christ. They should, in fact, be model citizens so that any charges of antisocial behavior would be proven false. They should be prepared to defend their views but do so in humility, not contrariness. Though they might experience ostracism

and constraints on their enjoyment of society's benefits, they should take heart knowing that they were truly citizens of a greater kingdom.

One way we can see 1 Peter addressing the situation is through its use of traditional codes of conduct for the household. These codes described the relative roles and duties of the members of the household and society. We see such codes clearly in Ephesians and Colossians. 1 Peter takes up this stock standard of behavioral duties and transforms it into a guide for members of the household of God. Whether the author intended for the readers to demonstrate their social conformity through such behavior or to solidify their identity as a distinct, semiseparate community has been debated. Overall, it appears that 1 Peter is aimed at building social cohesion within the church and providing its harassed members with a strong, hopeful sense of belonging to an elect body called to a higher standard of holy living, even at the price of misunderstanding and persecution. Even if their struggles should result in official "trials," they should faithfully follow the example of their Lord Jesus Christ.

THE MESSAGE OF 1 PETER

THE STRUCTURE OF THE BOOK

1 Peter is clearly a letter, unlike Hebrews or James. It has the typical parts of a letter: prescript, prayer, body, and epistolary closing. Attempts to see it as a composite of several earlier writings or a reworked edition of a baptismal or Passover liturgy have proven unsuccessful. The writing makes perfect sense as a letter written exactly as we have it and written for a specific purpose, as letters typically were. It does make much use of phrases and motifs that had become part of the emerging Christian tradition, and it draws heavily on Christian interpretations of the Old Testament, but the letter appears to be the creation of its author who was deeply concerned about the problems his readers faced. He wanted to give them a word of hope, strengthen their sense of community, and encourage them to be faithful in their suffering.

Observing these concerns gives us the following outline for 1 Peter:

Opening (1:1-9)
    Prescript (1:1-2)
    Prayer of Blessing (1:3-9)
The Hope of Pilgrims (1:10–2:10)
    Hope Anticipated (1:10-12)
    Hope in Action (1:13–2:3)
    Hope Actualized in Identity (2:4-10)

The Community of Pilgrims (2:11–3:12)
    Aliens and Exiles (2:11-12)
    Servants and Slaves (2:13-25)
    Wives and Husbands (3:1-7)
    All Pilgrims (3:8-12)
The Suffering of Pilgrims (3:13–5:11)
    Suffering after the Example of Christ (3:13–4:6)
    Suffering in Hope (4:7-19)
    Suffering in Humility (5:1-11)
Closing (5:12-14)

A SYNOPSIS OF THE THEMES

After assuring the readers in the opening address that they have been chosen and prepared by God for obedience, the author launches into a prayer of blessing (1:3-9) intended to introduce some of the themes the readers will be called to consider. First among these is the hope God has provided through the death and resurrection of Jesus. This hope assures the readers that despite their present trials they can rejoice even now, trusting that their hardships are part of God's purposes for the refinement of their faith.

The hope that pilgrims can enjoy in the present was anticipated by the prophets (1:10-12). Such a hope is not to be taken lightly by those who enjoy it; it compels them to holy living (1:13–2:13). This involves forsaking the lifestyle they had previously known. It calls them to love one another deeply and rid themselves of those behaviors that hinder love. They should realize who and what they are: a spiritual house built on the solid stone of Jesus (2:4-10). This stone that was rejected by the world is the foundation of their life as the chosen people of God. As God's chosen ones, they are called to be a holy, priestly people.

Living out who and what they are called to be compels them toward participation in a community that looks above for guidance (2:11–3:12). As resident aliens here below, they are called to represent their sovereign honorably. They should not earn the disrespect of those in the world by arrogantly flaunting their freedom from earthly standards and authorities, but rather they should exhibit the highest qualities of good citizenship (2:13-17). Using the structure of traditional household codes, the author speaks to those who as slaves are called to follow the example of Christ in humbly bearing the suffering inflicted upon them (2:18-25). He then addresses wives (3:1-6), urging them to exhibit modesty as they accept the authority of their husbands. Husbands, in turn, are to show proper respect toward their wives, who are joint heirs of hope with them (3:7). Then, all pilgrims are encouraged to cultivate the unity that allows them to experience the blessing of God (3:8-12).

The most specific concern of the book has to do with the suffering they can anticipate as faithful pilgrims and how they should respond to it (3:13–5:11). They are called to do good regardless of the cost, just as the righteous Christ suffered at the hands of and on behalf of the unrighteous (3:13–4:6). Though his goodness cost him his life, he was raised victoriously and will ultimately judge those who are unrighteous. Though they formerly followed the lifestyle of those around them, they can no longer do so. Their consciences must be clear, even when brought to trial, knowing that those who unjustly accuse them must one day account for their actions to the supreme judge.

As they endure suffering, they live in hope (4:7-19). They should expect trials, knowing that such trials signal the nearing end of this world. They should discipline themselves and help each other in the meantime. They should find joy in knowing that their sufferings on behalf of Christ are part of God's ultimate triumph.

Humility is to be the chief virtue expressed during their suffering (5:1-11). Those responsible for guiding the pilgrim community must exercise humility, and those who follow must also show a humble spirit. Above all, they should humble themselves to the guidance of God. They can trust in God's care and resist the temptation of the evil one. Ultimately, they can be assured that God will grant them the glory for which they live.

In closing, the author commends the faithfulness of Silvanus and reminds his readers that they do not serve and suffer alone (5:12-14).

Commentary

OPENING
(1:1-9)

PRESCRIPT
(1:1-2)

The first verse identifies the author simply as Peter, an apostle of Jesus Christ. No elaboration on his identity is given; presumably none was needed. The addressees, however, are described in detail both as to their location and as to their true identity. They live in several regions of Asia Minor (see the discussion above); thus they are rooted in a real time and place. More importantly, though, they have an eternal identity. They have been chosen and destined by God. They have been sanctified by the Spirit to live in obedience to Christ, by whose blood they have also been purified. The reference to Father, Spirit, and

Christ is not the full-blown Trinitarianism the church later developed, but it represents an early move in that direction.

PRAYER OF BLESSING
(1:3-9)

Letters typically had a prayer or blessing of some kind at this point. Usually they were brief and perfunctory. Paul developed his epistolary prayers as a way of introducing many of the themes he would treat in the body of his letters. 1 Peter follows Paul's pattern. The primary theme introduced here is hope (v. 3). The resurrection of Jesus from the dead has produced a "living" hope. The author assures the readers that they have been born into this hope, which carries with it the promise that they will inherit future glory. Nothing in this world can rob them of that inheritance. Thus, they can rejoice even now in the face of trials. In fact, the trials are a part of the process by which their faith is refined and their present experience of their future salvation is made more apparent. As pilgrims, they can trust that whatever suffering they endure will not adversely affect their ultimate destiny. They can live in hope.

THE HOPE OF PILGRIMS
(1:10–2:10)

HOPE ANTICIPATED
(1:10-12)

The salvation hope that enlivens them is to be understood as exactly what the prophets of old meant when they spoke of what was to come. This has been God's intention all along. When the author refers to the prophets inquiring about the person and time for realizing this salvation, he does not refer to specific Old Testament passages. His reference to "the sufferings destined for Christ," however, suggests that Isaiah was foremost in mind. Christians early on began to interpret the "Suffering Servant" passages in the second part of Isaiah in light of Jesus' own experience. While Jewish tradition understood such verses to refer to the nation of Israel or to the prophets themselves, who so often suffered for their faithful witness, Christians saw them as "predictions" of the cross of Christ. In this way, Christians appropriated the Jewish Scriptures and found a new key for understanding them. 1 Peter stresses that the prophets' words were intended to help his present readers. The prophets eagerly wanted to know something that even the angels longed to know, but their efforts were designed to serve those who had received the truth about God's provision of salvation in Christ.

HOPE IN ACTION
(1:13–2:3)

Because Christian pilgrims have received the truth about God's salvation, they are called to holy living. Hearing the "good news" brings heavy responsibility. Knowing what ultimately lies ahead obligates pilgrims now. They cannot live as they once did. Discipline, obedience, holy conduct are required. God's call to holiness in Leviticus 19, originally applied to Israel, has now become the summons for the pilgrims living in exile.

1 Peter 1:17 gives a clear depiction of the Christian life as one of pilgrimage. "The time of your exile" refers to the earthly life of pilgrims. The language of the Old Testament that described the plight of the people of Judah taken forcibly to live outside the promised land in Babylonia has here become a symbol of Christian existence. The words of the song, "This world is not my home; I'm just passing through," captures the sense of the symbol. 1 Peter, however, refuses to discount the significance of what pilgrims do as they "pass through." During "the time of exile" pilgrims have serious obligation. "Reverent" fear is advocated.

The means by which God uprooted them from the futile ways they had inherited from their ancestors and transformed them into exiles was the "precious blood of Christ" (v. 19). That cannot be taken lightly. God planned this all along (v. 20), but it was always intended for them in the last days. They have heard this good news, and they should trust that it is an imperishable word (v. 23). Thus, they must live fully in the love that characterizes the new life into which they have been born (v. 22). They have been born anew, but they still have growing to do. The salvation God prepared for them is not yet fully realized; they must grow into it (2:2). Pilgrimage is a process of actualizing the living hope through holy action.

HOPE ACTUALIZED IN IDENTITY
(2:4-10)

Actualizing the hope is rooted in a clear sense of identity. Pilgrims comprise the household of God. They are the "living" stones of God's spiritual house, built upon the living stone rejected by worldly builders. The building imagery here roots in several motifs. One is that of the people of God as a holy temple in which the spirit of God dwells. Ephesians 2:21-22 paints a similar picture of the people of God. Here, passages from Isaiah (18:16; 8:14-15) and the Psalms (118:22) are used to show that the Christ who was rejected and suffered has both become a stumbling block to those who rejected him and has become the cornerstone for those who have accepted him and become a part of

God's spiritual house. The temple imagery gets blended with the picture of these living stones serving as a holy priesthood (2:5, 9).

Another motif also lies behind the imagery of the church as God's house. This is a theme also found in Ephesians 2 (and in Colossians and 1 Timothy) of the church as a household (*oikos*). The household was the basic unit of ancient society. In Greek and Roman times philosophers gave much attention to how the household should be ordered (*oikonomia* = household law). Aristotle and others saw the stability of the household as the key to understanding the proper governance of the city-state. Often they would discuss politics or ethics in terms of household imagery. New Testament writers (especially of Ephesians and Colossians) adopted this tactic of using household imagery to develop other themes. 1 Peter does the same. In the discussion of the community of pilgrims that follows in 2:11–3:12 the household image is used to discuss the proper behavior of those in God's house.

As God's household, pilgrims have come to the living stone and have not rejected it. They have been drawn out of the futile ways of their past to form a chosen race, a royal priesthood, a holy nation (2:9). Labels that once stood as the pride of Israel are now applied to the church. Drawing from Exodus 19:6 and Hosea 2:23, the author depicts the church as the special possession of God, created out of the nothingness of their previous existence to become a suitable habitation for God's spirit.

THE COMMUNITY OF PILGRIMS
(2:11–3:12)

ALIENS AND EXILES
(2:11-12)

As members of the household of God, pilgrims are to distance themselves from the kinds of loyalties to the world that would indicate they were being governed by the flesh and not God's spirit. They are to live as "aliens" (*paroikoi*) and "exiles" (*parepidēmoi*). The terms had political connotations, but here they are used theologically. While some of the readers may, in fact, have been "homeless" in a political sense, others within the churches addressed appear to have been firmly rooted in the political and social systems of their various locations. It may also have been true that certain privileges belonging to political citizenship may have become unavailable, either by choice or by coercion, for some of the Christians involved. The terms, however, refer here to their true identity as residents of the household of God, a citizenship considered superior to any other communal ties. As "heavenly" citizens residing below, they are to conduct themselves as credible representatives of the sovereign they affirm so that even those who live outside the household will glorify the God for whom the aliens live.

Servants and Slaves
(2:13-25)

Faithfully representing God on earth means being good members of human society. This means accepting the human authorities that exist, even the emperor and his legates. They are servants (*douloi*) of God and are free people, not enslaved. Yet they are honor-bound to submit to earthly authority so as to bring no shame upon themselves or their master from those with whom they live. Treason was a popular charge against troublemakers. Already under suspicion because of their peculiar, exclusive loyalty to the Lord, the Christians could easily become the target of those needing scapegoats to explain why the crops had failed. Challenging the divine hierarchy that was thought to ensure divine blessing was grounds for legal action in their setting. Similarly, many today attribute the perceived decline in social morals to the rejection of established authorities by the young. The writer here wanted such accusations to be proven groundless.

One role within the standard household code gets special treatment: slaves (*oiketai*). The term used here is of "household" slaves. One could argue that slaves who had heard the liberating word of the gospel might be especially inclined to challenge the authority of their earthly masters. More probably, the image of the slave, which so often in the New Testament is a label Christian leaders applied to themselves as slaves of Christ, provided the best example of one living under worldly authority. Slaves were at the bottom rung of the social ladder. *Oiketai* were the lowest members of the oikos. The model of the slave voluntarily submitting even to a cruel master was an appropriate example for all Christians.

The supreme example of voluntary submission, though, was found in Christ (2:21-24). He suffered though he did no wrong. Christian household slaves, whether actually slaves or only symbolically so, are called to be equally guiltless to the charges that might be brought against them.

Wives and Husbands
(3:1-7)

Moving to another traditionally subordinate member of the household code, 1 Peter admonishes the wives likewise to submit to their husbands' authority. The option of challenging the assumed authority of the free, adult male was not even in the picture in their culture. The few instances where such challenges had occurred became historical scandals. Within that thoroughly male-dominated system the author urged compliance with the cultural norms—with one interesting difference. The wives are addressed as response-able persons: they are spoken to directly and instructed to submit. In nonbiblical uses of the household code, only free, adult males are addressed, because only such persons were considered capable of responsibility for their own actions. Here, wives are acknowledged as having the willful capacity to shape their behavior so that they are perceived as models of virtue. The wife who obeys the word (of God) may "without a word" win over those husbands who do not obey the word (of God). The wives, thusly, are told to adopt simple attire that allows their inner virtue to be seen. Abraham's wife is their example. The thrust here is that wives are to function within the male-dominated system without becoming a source of criticism by those outside the church. Powerlessness to change the system then should not be taken to condemn wives to male domination in systems that have begun to recognize the inherent injustice of gender-based (or race-based) social structures.

The other member of the wife-husband pair in the household code also receives instruction. Husbands are to show honor to their wives. The presupposition is condescending—as the "weaker sex"—but the intention again is to preserve peace and stability in the household. Turbulent households would substantiate the outsiders' charges that Christians were subversive. At least, the husband is called to recognize the wife as a fellow heir of God's gracious gift of life.

ALL PILGRIMS
(3:8-12)

Departing from the standard form of the household code, the author then addresses the whole church. Humility is encouraged for all and should be engendered in sympathy and tenderness and expressed through unity of spirit and love for one another. The call to non-retaliation in the face of abuse echoes Jesus' words in the Sermon on the Mount (Matt 5:39-41). The section concludes with a lengthy quotation from Psalm 34. It reinforces the general theme that those in the household of God are to turn from evil and do good.

The Suffering of Pilgrims
(3:13–5:11)

Suffering after the Example of Christ
(3:13–4:6)

The theme of bearing suffering in the face of unjust persecution, which has been touched upon in several places earlier, receives fuller treatment in the last major section of the letter. The whole section contains two main passages of instruction for the readers (3:13-17 and 4:1-5), each of which is supported by a reference to the example of Christ (3:18-22 and 4:6). The two supporting segments contain some of the most perplexing words in the New Testament.

The first section begins with a question: "Who will harm you if you are eager to do good?" The question would seem to suggest a simple, negative answer: "Why, no one, of course!" But the author knows that better. Those who do good can and do suffer harm. Thus he states that even when unjust suffering happens, one should feel blessed. Such unjust abuse may come, but the pilgrim should not shrink back in fear. Instead, one should be ready to give a defense for the hope possessed. The term for defense here is *apologia*. It suggests legal proceedings, and, in fact, the setting where one might have to give a defense could very well be a formal hearing before an official. The term could also refer to nonpublic deliberations with anyone who questioned a Christian's peculiar lifestyle. Having to explain why one refused to participate in the common activities of ancient life could come in any number of times and places.

What is significant here is that the believer is urged to be prepared to make such a defense, not to withhold an accounting of the reasons for being different. In contrast to most other groups that appeared strange to the outsider, Christians are being urged not to keep their beliefs a secret. Christians are to be open and honest. Furthermore, this defense should be given with gentleness and reverence, not abrasively or arrogantly. The manner of witnessing to the gospel is here considered an important part of the witness itself. Belief is not to be isolated from behavior. By their good behavior, Christians can hope to counter the slander of their beliefs. If they still have to suffer, at least they suffer with a good conscience knowing that they have done no wrong.

Here again the example of Christ as one who suffered though he had done no wrong is employed. But here the point is taken beyond example to emphasize the result of Christ's suffering. He was put to death in the flesh, as they may also be put to death. But he was made alive in the spirit. At this point a puzzling assertion is made that it was "in the spirit" that Christ went and made a proclamation to the spirits in prison (3:19). These spirits are described as those who did not obey during the time that Noah was building the ark. The reference to Noah's ark leads to an allegorical interpretation of the water through which Noah and his sons passed linking it to the water of baptism through which Christians pass (3:20-21). The baptism is effective not because it cleanses the body but because it enables the cleansing of the conscience before God.

The problematic part of this section has to do with the preaching to the enslaved spirits. One common understanding is that this occurred when Jesus descended into the realm of death between the crucifixion and the resurrection. The spirits are thus often seen as those persons who had died in the flood and who were given a chance to repent by Christ. Others see the spirits not as human spirits but rather evil spirits who have been imprisoned by God. In this case, Christ is seen to have preached judgment, not salvation. Either version of this view has led to the idea of Jesus descending into hell, which is affirmed in some versions of the Apostles Creed.

Another way to understand this reference, though, is to see it in connection with Jesus' ascension. Death, resurrection, and ascension are clearly seen in 1 Peter, but the idea of a descent into hell is not. Nor is it clear that any place in the New Testament refers to dead persons as "spirits." A common view about evil spirits, especially in Asia Minor (see Ephesians and Colossians), was that the astral beings (stars) of the sky were entrapped spirits who often tried to harm those below. They were the principalities and powers of the air who were feared by the bulk of the population and who needed to be appeased to avoid their harmful actions. In this view, Jesus, though innocently killed, was raised up and proclaimed his triumph over all evil powers as he ascended up to the Father. The point would be that just as the righteous Jesus triumphed over suffering and death, those who suffer for righteousness' sake can expect vindication over all unjust powers.

Christ's example in suffering leads to the second unit of instruction (4:1-5) for the readers. As Christ suffered in the flesh, they should be prepared to suffer during their time "in the flesh" without giving in to human desires. Though they had previously known well the life of indulging such desires, they had turned from that. Their transformation had earned them the criticism and judgment of their former friends, but they could find encouragement knowing that those friends who were still trapped in desire would have to defend their lifestyles before the supreme judge.

The reference to God's judgment leads to the second puzzling passage (4:6). The dead had had the gospel proclaimed to them. At first glance, this seems to support the idea that Jesus had preached to the dead spirits of humans. Since the verb for preaching here specifically refers to "proclaiming the gospel," the idea would be that Jesus gave the dead a chance to respond. Here, though, the dead are not spirits;

they are among the living and the dead judged by God. They are most likely to be seen as those Christians who had died, perhaps through persecution, who had heard the gospel. They had been judged in the flesh by the world, but they had been made alive "in the spirit" by God. Just as Jesus had been put to death "in the flesh" and made alive "in the spirit," they had passed through the negative judgment of the powers that be in this world but had received the positive judgment of the one true Judge.

SUFFERING IN HOPE
(4:7-19)

The suffering of pilgrims is then set in an eschatological context: "The end of all things is near." Because the end is near, Christians should strengthen one another for their times of trial. They should discipline themselves, maintain constant love for one another, be hospitable to one another, and serve one another. Words and actions should be seen as the gifts of God and should be used for God's glory.

They should also understand that their trials are a normal part of the ending of the present age. Apocalyptic language is subdued in 1 Peter, but the apocalyptic view that the people of God are engaged in a dangerous struggle with evil underlies the conviction that the faithful should expect to endure increased suffering before the final act of history. Should Christians have to suffer for being called a "Christian," they should rejoice because that proves that they are exhibiting the character of Christ. Here we have the only instance of the term Christian being used in the New Testament apart from the two references in the book of Acts. Again, they are told that they should never be guilty of a crime that is legitimately punishable. But suffering for the name of Christ is an honor. The sifting of the faithful that such suffering brings is a kind of judgment on the household of God itself. It clearly separates the faithful pilgrims from the unfaithful. And if pilgrims can expect such judgment, then what about the judgment that will fall upon those who make no claim to the household of God? Pilgrims can endure their suffering, though it is unjust, by trusting God for their ultimate salvation and striving to do good in the meantime.

SUFFERING IN HUMILITY
(5:1-11)

The final section focuses on the internal life of the community of faith. Humility should guide their interaction with fellow pilgrims, just as it should guide their dealings with those outside the church. Leaders, here called elders, should exercise humility as they guide the flock of God. The author places himself in this group and adds that he is a witness to Christ's own suffering. Christ is seen as the chief shepherd, and those who follow his humble example as leaders will receive their reward from him.

Those who follow the lead of the elders must also exercise humility. A quotation from Proverbs 3:34 is used to support the point that God favors the humble. Humility ultimately means trusting in God's guidance. Concerns about the present trials can be turned over to God, for God will finally vindicate the faithful. Faithful pilgrims must stay alert in the meantime, guarding themselves against the clever efforts of the evil one to thwart them on their journey. They can find encouragement knowing that they have fellow travelers throughout the world, and by remembering that their trials are for only a short time in the grand scheme of things. In the end, the God of grace will secure their salvation.

CLOSING

(5:12-14)

The letter closes in standard fashion with a personal word from the author commending the faithfulness of Silvanus, presumably the carrier of the letter. It also contains a greeting from their sister church "in Babylon." Since Jews and Christians saw Rome as a kind of new Babylon, especially after the destruction of the temple in Jerusalem in A.D. 70, most interpreters take this reference to mean that the letter was written from Rome. The reference to Mark has been used to support the later tradition that Mark became an associate of Peter in Rome. The instruction to greet one another with a kiss and the prayer of peace at the end are often found in the letters of Paul.

FOR FURTHER READING

Achtemeier, Paul J. *1 Peter*. Hermeneia. Minneapolis: Fortress Press, 1996.

Balch, David L. *Let Wives Be Submissive: The Domestic Code in 1 Peter*. SBL Monograph Series. Chico CA: Scholars Press, 1981.

Best, Ernest. *1 Peter*. New Century Bible. Greenwood SC: Attic Press, 1971.

Davids, Peter H. *The First Epistle of Peter*. The New International Commentary on the New Testament. Grand Rapids: Wm. B. Eerdmans Publishing Co., 1990.

Elliott, John H. *Home for the Homeless: A Sociological Exegesis of 1 Peter, Its Structure and Strategy*. Philadelphia: Fortress Press, 1981.

Michaels, J. Ramsey. *1 Peter*. Word Biblical Commentary 49. Waco TX: Word Books, 1988.

Perkins, Pheme. *First and Second Peter, James, and Jude*. Interpretation. Louisville KY: John Knox Press, 1995.

Richard, Earl J. Reading *1 Peter, Jude, and 2 Peter*. Macon GA: Smyth & Helwys Publishing, Inc., 2000.

Chapter 4

Jude and 2 Peter
Warning Pilgrims about Misdirection

Introduction

THE PUZZLE OF JUDE AND 2 PETER

Both Jude and 2 Peter speak to the problem pilgrims face of losing direction on their journey. Both letters address the threat of misdirection that can come from outsiders whose teachings may lead the faithful astray. Both letters, therefore, give careful attention to correcting false ideas. Neither letter gives a full account of what those false ideas were, or who it was that espoused them. Instead, the authors tended to engage in the kind of personal assault that was common for religious and philosophical debates at the time. Within the polemical attacks on the "opponents," however, we can find clues about the specific problems that threatened to misdirect the church.

LATE ACCEPTANCE

Among the letters known as "Catholic Epistles," meaning that they are viewed as intended for the church at large, Jude and 2 Peter have always been stepchildren. Though technically "in the family," they have seldom been embraced with enthusiasm. Evidence from the early church indicates that they were late in arriving on the scene of treasured Christian writings that eventually emerged as the canon of New Testament Scriptures. They were not known in many areas of the church, and when they were known they were often objects of dispute.

The earliest use of Jude was by the author of 2 Peter, himself, as we shall see below. Toward the end of the second century, Clement of Alexandria and Tertullian both referred to Jude, and the Muratorian Fragment (probably from the same time) lists Jude among those writings accepted in the church. 2 Peter was not mentioned by any second-century writers, though it may have been used by the authors of the apocryphal books *Gospel of Peter* and *Apocalypse of Peter*.

The third-century writer Origen referred to Jude by name as a valuable writing but also said that he was aware of a second letter attributed to Peter that was generally doubted as to authenticity. His contemporary, Hippolytus, named Jude and 2 Peter as useful writings, but he did not consider them "scripture." By the early fourth century, the church had begun to distinguish between "acknowledged books" and "disputed books," as is shown by Eusebius in his *Ecclesiastical History* (ca. A.D. 325). Both Jude and 2 Peter were "disputed." By the middle of the fourth century, both books were generally included in the lists of books being supported as having canonical status, though the Syrian church resisted Jude, 2 Peter, and other disputed books on into the fifth century.

AUTHORSHIP

The matter of acceptance was often determined by judgments about authorship. Jude was seldom questioned, but the early church seldom viewed 2 Peter as having been written by the apostle. Only in recent times has belief that Peter wrote it become a test of faith in some quarters. The fact that 2 Peter refers to a collection of Paul's letters as "scripture" (3:16) and reflects knowledge of material from the Synoptic Gospels clearly puts its writing long after the days of Peter. The author's use of Jude also argues persuasively against 2 Peter's having been written by Peter. Both Jude and 2 Peter fit the context of the church's struggles in the late first or early second centuries. Thus, both are best understood as pseudonymous works intended to carry the apostolic message into the battle against new challenges. Rather than authorial deception, the authors were following the pattern of the day in providing the church with a continuing voice from its earliest leaders.

LITERARY RELATIONSHIP

Without question a direct literary relationship exists between Jude and 2 Peter. The only question is, which one uses the other. Those trying to argue for Petrine authorship of 2 Peter have labored to show that Jude used the apostle's second letter. The preponderance of evidence, however, leads to the opposite conclusion. (That is one reason Jude is being treated before 2 Peter in the synopsis and commentary below.) The most obvious places where 2 Peter depends on Jude are 2:1-18 (Jude 4-16) and 3:1-3 (Jude 17-18). While the material in Jude fits into a carefully constructed argument, the parts taken up in 2 Peter are clumsily worked into that author's argument. Jude's clear allusions to noncanonical writings, such as *1 Enoch*, are deleted in 2 Peter when those sections are used, presumably because referring to such writings would have played into the hands of his opponents. The use of Jude by the author of 2 Peter, as well as his reference to Gospel material and the writings of Paul, indicate that the author was well-versed in early Christian literature. The developed writing style also shows that the author had a solid educational background.

THE SETTING OF JUDE AND 2 PETER

HISTORICAL SETTING

Modesty must guide any attempt to place these two writings in a specific time or place. We simply do not have enough information. Traditional views about authorship require dating them near the middle of the first century, but that period does not match the concerns of the letters at all. We have to go later. How much later is the question. Some date 2 Peter very late, even to A.D. 160, but they do so largely because they see the "heresy" he was attacking as Gnosticism. While the roots of Gnosticism are obscure, the full-blown Gnostic heresy arose only after the middle of the second century.

Other deviant viewpoints besides Gnosticism better fit the concerns of both 2 Peter and Jude. The author of Jude reacts to people who have come into the church and questioned its teachings about the return of Christ. That scenario could fit into any time after the first generation of Christians had passed from the scene and hopes in an early return were beginning to dwindle. Near the end of the first century the church had to deal with this issue. Since Jude is taken here to precede 2 Peter, then 2 Peter most likely fits better in the early second century. The author's knowledge of and reaction to certain philosophical ideas that were popular then also makes the first two decades of the second century a good possibility.

THEOLOGICAL SETTING

While we cannot know the time or place of these writings, we can learn something about the theological concerns of the authors. Jude is directed against intruders who have questioned the reliability of the church's teaching about the future. This is perceived by the author as an arrogant challenge to the authority of God. Thus, he strives to show in various ways that the church's message is true and that those who deny it have sealed their own doom.

2 Peter is more complex. The author did not actually say that false teachers had come into the church. Rather, he seems to have been preparing his readers for erroneous ideas that he knew were circulating. These subversive ideas had to do with the second coming, as in Jude, but a deeper issue also was at stake: the providence of God. The

Christian belief in the second coming was tied to their conviction that God was in control of history and would one day bring it to its appointed conclusion.

Jerome Neyrey has pointed out that the philosophical movement known as Epicureanism was well-known in antiquity for questioning the divine guidance of the universe. They held that persons were totally free to determine their own destinies because no God or gods existed behind the scenes. They affirmed a purely materialistic view of life, holding that the person was composed of atomic particles that disintegrated at death. Hence, there was no eternal fate because there was no soul or spirit. Epicurean ideas found a hearing in the Greco-Roman world even among those who were not Epicureans. In fact, their reputation for questioning divine providence was so well known that the Jewish historian Josephus likened the Sadducees to Epicureans because of their disbelief in fate and the resurrection. The name "Epicurean" is very similar to the term *apikoros*, which is generally translated "scoffer." While Epicureanism may not have been the particular threat, "scoffers" is exactly what 2 Peter calls the proponents of the false teaching (3:3). Their questioning of God's control of human history was the basic concern. This scoffing seems to have focused on Christian teachings about the future, passing them off as "myths." Thus, the author argued that such teachings are well-founded in traditions, scriptures, and other authorities that his readers knew to be reliable.

The efforts of both Jude and 2 Peter to maintain the future-orientation of pilgrims on the way has much to say to the modern church about the danger of losing sight of the gospel's vision of a world ultimately transformed by the power of God. Reducing the Christian message of hope to a personalized quest for fulfillment alienates pilgrims from the larger vision of God's activity in the world at large.

THE MESSAGES OF JUDE AND 2 PETER

THE STRUCTURES OF THE BOOKS

Jude

The structure of Jude shows evidence of being influenced by ancient standards of rhetoric. Rhetoric was viewed as the art of persuasion, an important objective for both speech and writing. Philosophers and rhetoricians devoted much attention to prescribing particular forms of argumentation that would accomplish specific objectives in different settings. In general, rhetorical arguments were structured to lead people to believe or not believe certain things or to do or not do certain things. Various terms were used in antiquity to define the parts of a rhetorical argument, but they basically included these elements: (1) a *beginning* that established a connection between the speaker/writer and the audience; (2) a *narration* of why the argument must be made; (3) a statement of the *main point* to be argued; (4) a string of *proofs* to support the main point; and (5) a *summation* of the main point. The different parts could be combined, especially if the argument was in the form of a letter.

An outline of Jude that takes into consideration the rhetorical design of the letter is given below.

Prescript (1-2)
   [used as the beginning establishing a connection with readers]
Body of the Letter (3-23)
   Narration and Main Point (3-4)
   Proofs (5-16)
   Summation (17-23)
Benediction (24-25)
   [used to support the summation]

2 Peter

The structure of 2 Peter, likewise, reveals that the author was well-versed in ancient rhetoric. In fact, the rhetorical design is very complex, representing a more thorough mastery of the art of persuasion than Jude. All the main features of a standard rhetorical argument are present in 2 Peter, but they are woven together in a very different fashion that suggests the author was deliberately trying to counter arguments that his readers had either heard or would likely hear. So, instead of a main point being stated and then proven, we find first an extended attempt to strengthen the bond between author and audience (1:3-15) and then a series of contrasts between what the supposed opponents might say and what our author explains to be the truth (1:16–3:13).

Detailed analysis of the argument could give us a complicated outline with many more points and subpoints than the one offered below. The following outline is, however, intended to be a helpful device for following the main flow of the rhetorical argument.

Prescript (1:1-2)
Beginning (1:3-15)
   [used to establish a connection with readers]
   Affirmation of God's Gifts (1:3-4)
   The Proper Response (1:5-11)
   The Apostle's Final Word (1:12-15)

The Argument (1:16–3:13)
    Christ's Coming Is No Myth (1:16-21)
    False Prophets Will Be Judged (2:1-22)
    God's Judgment Will Surely Come (3:1-13)
Summation (3:14-18)
    Recapitulation (3:14-16)
    Final Appeal (3:17-18)

A SYNOPSIS OF THE THEMES

Jude

The letter of Jude has basically one theme: contending for the true faith against those who would mislead the faithful. This theme is worked out mostly in a denunciation of false Christians who have infiltrated the ranks of the readers. This denunciation includes a rhetorical argument that shows first of all that God has always dealt harshly with such threats to true faith. The examples of the unfaithful members of the Exodus generation, the rebellious angels, and the immoral of Sodom and Gomorrah, all of whom met divine punishment, are given. Then the author associates the present threat with the ancient ones and likens them to other notorious villains (the devil, Cain, Balaam, Korah). He notes that such dangerous intruders were predicted by Enoch and by the apostles. He admonishes the readers to keep themselves pure from the intruders' influence while showing mercy to those who have been swayed by them. The closing benediction is an assurance that God will preserve them in this struggle.

2 Peter

The concern of 2 Peter is primarily to counter denials that were circulating about the coming judgment of God. The author wants his readers to know that what they had already been taught was true, despite the arguments they might hear to the contrary. Thus, 2 Peter begins the defense of traditional teaching by affirming its goodness as a gift from God. The goodness of the knowledge passed on to his readers must be lived out in their lives, however, as a guard against those who challenge the truth.

Peter, himself, is one argument supporting the truth of the received faith, both because of his acknowledged authority and because of his experience of the transfiguration glory of the coming Christ. Thus, the message of God's coming judgment is not rooted in myth but in the prophetic word confirmed in Jesus.

False teachers will undoubtedly question this truth, and many will follow them. But they will meet their own destruction in the end, as did those in the past who challenged God (evil angels, Noah's generation, Sodom and Gomorrah). Those who accept the truth can be assured of the same kind of protection that God gave to Lot. Those who reject it, however, are exposing their own enslavement to corruption and will ultimately be exposed as the worthless persons they are. Though they should know better, since they have heard the truth, they have sealed their own fate.

Scoffing at God's governance of the world and denying the reality of judgment ignores the evidence that proves God's power. Such arguments also reveal a basic misunderstanding about the nature of God, especially God's patience. God will destroy the world by fire and the godless will be consumed, though the timing of the end remains unknown. Those who believe the truth are called to live in obedient expectation of the end of this world and the creation of a new one.

Therefore, those who wait in faith must attend to their own condition, as Paul had instructed in his letters, even though his teachings have often been twisted. Furthermore, the faithful must resist the error of the false teachers, growing in the grace and knowledge of the Lord.

Commentary: Jude

PRESCRIPT
(1-2)

The letter identifies its sender as Jude (Greek *Ioudas*), a servant of Jesus Christ and a brother of James. The self-designation of the author as a "servant" (*doulos*) resembles the simple title taken by the author of James and may suggest some knowledge of that writing, especially since James is also mentioned here. Servant was, however, a common title taken by early Christian leaders. Matthew 13:55 and Mark 6:3 name a Judas (*Iuodas*) along with James as brothers of Jesus. A later tradition, preserved by Eusebius, tells of how Jude's sons were brought before the Roman emperor Domitian. Otherwise, we have no information about him. The lack of claim to kinship with Jesus while affirming it with James may be due to reluctance to suggest even remotely any kind of equality with Jesus. Mentioning the well-known James, however, strengthens the author's claim to apostolic authority.

The identification of the addressees brings the first of many triplets used by the author. His readers are called, beloved, and kept. No more specific identity is given, indicating that the letter may have been intended for Christians in general. They are beloved in God the Father, a quality the writer stresses several times. And they are kept for Jesus Christ, a reminder that the readers have a destiny that awaits them and for which they are being preserved as they struggle against misdirection.

Verse 2 departs from the standard greeting somewhat, resembling a prayer like those one would expect after the greeting.

BODY OF THE LETTER
(3-23)

NARRATION AND MAIN POINT
(3-4)

Calling them "Beloved," the author begins his argument by explaining that, while he had intended to write them another kind of letter that discussed their common salvation, the present problem has compelled him to address an urgent threat to their shared faith. The term "Beloved," along with his triple identification of them in the prescript establishes a close connection between writer and reader. He is one of them, not an outsider. He is concerned about their bond, however, and must urge them to contend for the faith they hold in common. Faith here is not viewed in the dynamic way it is in Paul's letters. Instead, faith is seen more as a depository of beliefs and accepted practices given to the church.

This rule of faith, as it later came to be called in the church, was being threatened by persons the author labels "intruders," thereby indicating that they are not truly "of us." Three charges are made against them here at the start: they have already been condemned as ungodly, they pervert the grace of God into licentiousness, and they deny the Lord Jesus in some way. The idea that their judgment has in some sense already been fixed and the criticism of their behavior come into play again in the rest of the argument. Exactly how they were denying Jesus, though, is never explained. It is probably rooted in their questioning of God's coming rule of all things through Jesus. Their presence as a threat that must be resisted provides the main point for the case developed against them.

PROOFS
(5-16)

The series of proofs employed to support the contention that they are a dangerous threat begins with a reminder of something the readers supposedly already knew, a typical rhetorical device. Three instances of God's judgment on threats to the well-being of God's people are named. The first is the case of those Hebrews rescued by God from slavery in Egypt who were later destroyed because of their unbelief. That this example from Numbers 14 (cf. Ps 95) was a well-established traditional warning against wavering in the faith is borne out by its extensive treatment in Hebrews 3:7–4:11. The case of the immoral residents of Sodom and Gomorrah being destroyed by God was also a familiar piece of scripture (Gen 19). The story about the fallen angels, however, is only loosely based on Genesis 6:1-4. It draws more directly on the development of that incident in the book of Enoch (1 Enoch 6–16), an apocalyptic writing from around the second century B.C. that was influential for many Jews and Christians. Later (v. 14), Jude quotes directly from this book. All of these examples show the punishment that awaits those who rebel against the rule of God.

The author then connects the present threat to the ancient ones. The "intruders" also defile the flesh (as did the people of Sodom and Gomorrah and the evil angels who took human women as wives) and reject authority (as did the angels and the rebellious Hebrews). The charge that they also "slander the glorious ones" is more puzzling. Most likely, the "glorious ones" are the angels who were understood to preserve God's moral order. The intruders (as did the people of Sodom and Gomorrah and the evil angels) have challenged God's moral rule, apparently in their licentious behavior.

The charge of slander appears to be the major crime of the intruders. Thus, their behavior is contrasted with that of the chief "glorious one," the angel Michael. The story of Michael contending with the devil over Moses' body is not in Scripture, but was drawn from Jewish tradition that now exists literarily in only fragmentary texts. The point of the story here is that Michael refused to indulge in slander, even against the devil. The intruders, however, slander everything they do not understand. Exactly what it is they do not understand is unclear. They clearly do understand their animal instincts, however, and have no problem following them. Again, it appears that the intruders were questioning the need for moral principles, and that they ridiculed the arguments Jude and others accepted that based such moral principles on the natural order of the world as created by God and maintained by God's angels. The inevitable end of such subverters is to be seen in the triple example of Cain, Balaam, and Korah, all of whom in some way questioned God's rule.

Jude then castigates and caricatures the opponents. They are blemishes on the love feasts, the Agape meals that early Christians observed as a sign of their unity and of their hope in partaking of the messianic banquet. They are waterless clouds, fruitless trees, wild waves, and wandering stars. The first three images depict uselessness. The stars "for whom the deepest darkness has been preserved" again connects them with the punishment of the rebellious angels, according to 1 Enoch.

The author finally appeals directly to the book of Enoch (v. 14). He quotes 1 Enoch 1:9, which describes the coming destruction of the wicked ones by the holy angels. Jude includes the intruders among those to be destroyed. He criticizes their "indulgence in their own lusts" without specifying what lustful things they did. He is more clear in denouncing their grumbling, malcontent, and bombastic and flattering speech. Again, their major crime seems to have been in questioning cherished beliefs and thereby causing disorder.

SUMMATION
(17-23)

In bringing his argument to a close, Jude returns to calling his readers "Beloved." Twice he does so (vv. 17, 20). The first time, he reminds the readers of more recent testimony to the threat presented by the intruders, that of the apostles themselves. They predicted that such scoffers would arise. What they spoke of has happened in these people, Jude asserts. They do not possess the Spirit, and thus cause senseless division with their challenges to "the faith once for all entrusted to the saints."

The second time he calls them beloved, Jude encourages his readers to hold to the entrusted faith and be built up by it. Having the Spirit, they should pray in it. They should live in love and trust in Christ's coming mercy. Difficult as it may be to do, they should also show mercy to those affected by the intruders, striving to return them to the fold, while steering clear of defilement by their outer behavior ("hating their tunics"). The extension of mercy does not seem to include the perpetrators themselves.

BENEDICTION
(24-25)

The letter lacks the typical closing. Instead we find a moving benediction that affirms the power of God to keep the readers untarnished by the threat of the intruders. The inclusion here of language stressing the glory and eternal authority of God gives a final response to those who have questioned the divine scheme of things.

Commentary: 2 Peter

PRESCRIPT
(1:1-2)

The writer identifies himself as Simeon Peter. *Simeon* is a direct transliteration into Greek of the Aramaic name that was usually assimilated to the similar Greek name *Simon*. In Acts 15:14 James calls Peter *Simeon*; otherwise he is always referred to as Peter, Cephas, or Simon Peter. The use of the more Hebraic form may suggest the author came from a Jewish Christian group. Simeon Peter is simply called a servant and apostle here.

The letter is sent to those who share the faith of the identified sender. This identification serves to create a bond between sender and recipients. What he has to say is rooted in a faith they have in common.

The greeting merges with prayer (as in Jude). The grace and peace prayed for is in the "knowledge" of God and Jesus. This knowledge is something they already have, but the author is concerned that they trust this knowledge, which is being challenged, and grow in it.

BEGINNING
(1:3-15)

AFFIRMATION OF GOD'S GIFTS
(1:3-4)

The place normally held by a thanksgiving prayer in letters is given to a kind of announcement. God has given to the readers what they need to make it through this life and prepare for the life to come. Specifically, they have been given the knowledge of God's promises. They know what lies ahead for them. This knowledge can set them free from the world's corruption so that they can share in the divine glory. Assuring his readers that what they have been told about the future is something they can rely on is the primary concern of this letter.

THE PROPER RESPONSE
(1:5-11)

This knowledge carries responsibility. They must live it out by supporting their faith with goodness and a series of other virtues, all of which involve growing in assurance and in fulfillment of their faith. Growing in these virtues is a sure guard against being misdirected. It makes their knowledge fruitful and not empty. If they neglect to grow in this knowledge, they are exposing their own lack of appreciation for the transformation that God has performed in them. If they confirm through their maturing God's call and election, then they will not have to worry about being misled.

THE APOSTLE'S FINAL WORD
(1:12-15)

To help them grow in their received knowledge, the "sender" of the letter issues what is to be for them a constant reminder of what they already know. The use of reminder and memory here is a typical rhetorical device. The message from Peter is to have a continuing function as his final testimony. This device of a "last will and testament" was a common literary tool. It signified that the writing itself was to be received as an authoritative last word. Here it reinforces the teaching they have received by connecting it to apostolic authority, best represented in the person of Peter. "Peter" says he has received from Jesus a revelation that his death is near. He will not leave, however, without giving them this message to support their faith.

THE ARGUMENT
(1:16–3:13)

CHRIST'S COMING IS NO MYTH
(1:16-21)

The portrait of Peter giving his last reminder leads into the first refutation of false teaching that concerns the author. As if in anticipation that they would hear (or had already heard) people questioning the Christian idea of the second coming, he assures them that he and the other apostolic teachers had not been spreading myths. A common tactic of Epicureans and those influenced by them was to ridicule stories about divine beings and their creation and control of the world. Peter uses personal testimony to confirm the validity of the teaching about Christ's coming by asserting that he had already seen the glorified Lord on the mountain. This is a clear allusion to the Transfiguration account found in the Synoptic Gospels. It presupposes that the readers would have known the story. There Jesus had received the affirmation of God, so they can trust that God will, indeed, bring Jesus back in glory, as he had said.

Since the prophetic message has already been confirmed by this well-attested event, the readers should trust in it as a beacon guiding them through dark days. This confirmed prophecy is of God, not humans. The interpretation of the event likewise is no individual human invention. They can trust the word.

FALSE PROPHETS WILL BE JUDGED
(2:1-22)

Predictably, though, some will not trust the word. False prophets arose in Old Testament days, and they should be expected in the present. 2 Peter does not say that they have already arrived among his readers, but if not, they will. They will bring in destructive ideas, even denying the *Master*. What they will deny is the sovereignty of God, that there is a God in control. They will be deceptive and persuasive, but their efforts will only earn them God's punishment.

In support of his contention that the false teachers will meet their doom, the author draws on Jude. He names the same groups that received divine retribution (angels, Noah's generation, Sodom and Gomorrah), but he deletes the part in Jude about the angels that was directly taken from *1 Enoch*. The book of Enoch was exactly the kind of work the opponents would ridicule. Instead, the author adds a positive example about God's deliverance of Lot as a sign that God will rescue those who faithfully resist the onslaught of wickedness.

The characterization of the false teachers as wicked employs the kinds of vices that writers typically used in polemical debates. Especially criticized here is their use of slander. Omitting Jude's allusion to the apocryphal story of Michael wrestling with the devil over Moses' body, the author nonetheless accuses the villains of even slandering the angels, probably through questioning their existence. Continuing to follow the pattern of Jude's argument, he inserts charges outlining the opponents' immorality. They ridicule what they do not understand; indeed, they cannot understand it because they are trapped in the lusts of this world.

In the end the opponents are empty and futile. They promise freedom, but are enslaved and lead others to enslavement. Here we see a reflection of the claims of Epicureanlike teachers, asserting their freedom from external authority, especially divine, as they pursue their self-chosen paths. Preaching freedom, they live in slavery made all the worse because they have heard the truth that could really set them free. Having heard it and turned from it, they are in worse shape than if they had never heard it. Knowing the truth but disbelieving it renders them impenetrable to the truth's power to save. Proverbs 26:11 is quoted as a pitiable and laughable portrait of condition.

GOD'S JUDGMENT WILL SURELY COME
(3:1-13)

The author makes another claim to Petrine authority by referring to this letter as his second. This presupposes some awareness of another letter attributed to Peter, probably 1 Peter. This second letter is another reminder to them that they should heed the message of the prophets and apostles they have already received. As predicted already, scoffers (*apikoroi*) will come. These scoffers will challenge their traditions and convictions. Specifically, they will question the traditions about the second coming. Those traditions affirmed the triumph of God over evil and attested to God's control of history. The failure of the second coming to occur was proof to the scoffers that it would not occur, that the traditions were only nonsense. Things stood as they always had, an Epicurean argument against the intervention by God in human affairs.

What these scoffers do, the author argues, is ignore the clear teaching of Scripture about God's involvement with the world. God created the world. God also destroyed the world once with water. God has also kept the world going until the time appointed for its destruction by fire. Another philosophical tradition, Stoicism, held that the world existed in cycles, each of which came to a fiery conclusion before the next began. The Stoic view, which was more widely held than the Epicurean, was more compatible with the Christian in this respect. Hence, the Stoic image of a fiery end was useful to the author.

The point of the image of fiery destruction and of the following argument was that God was patiently maintaining the world until the time of judgment. Judgment's delay must not be construed as a sign that it will not come or that God is not in control. Rather, humans should realize that God operates on a different timetable. God's tardiness is itself a sign of divine longing for all people to repent and be saved. When God is good and ready, the end will come quickly, as a thief in the night (as Jesus and Paul had said; Matt 24:43; Luke 12:39; 1 Thess 5:2).

SUMMATION
(3:14-18)

RECAPITULATION
(3:14-16)

The argument concludes with a recapitulation of the main thrust and an appeal to Paul. The readers should wait for what they have heard to be verified, as it will. While waiting they are to keep themselves on track. Paul had said the same thing in his letters, our author notes. He refers to a collection of Paul's letters and places them on the same level as other scriptures. This reference suggests that our author was writing some time after Paul and Peter, long enough after for Paul's letters to have been collected and circulated and recognized widely as an authoritative word. The end of the first century is probably the earliest that such would have occurred. The author also noted that some persons had misconstrued Paul's words, even using them, perhaps, to argue against the second coming.

FINAL APPEAL
(3:17-18)

The final appeal reminds the readers again that they already know the truth; they have been forewarned. Thus, they should be prepared to resist the arguments to the contrary that they might encounter. Again, they are urged to grow in the grace and knowledge given to them by God. The final benediction is a tribute to the One who has glory already and who holds the future.

FOR FURTHER READING

Bauckham, Richard J. *Jude, 2 Peter*. Word Biblical Commentary 50. Waco TX: Word Books, 1983.

Broadhead, Edwin K. "Second Peter." *Mercer Commentary on the Bible.* Macon GA: Mercer University Press, 1995.

Mills, Watson E. "Jude." *Mercer Commentary on the Bible.* Macon GA: Mercer University Press, 1995.

Neyrey, Jerome H. *2 Peter, Jude*. Anchor Bible 37C. New York: Doubleday, 1993.

Perkins, Pheme. *First and Second Peter, James, and Jude.* Interpretation. Louisville KY: John Knox Press, 1995.

Richard, Earl J. *Reading 1 Peter, Jude, and 2 Peter.* Macon GA: Smyth & Helwys Publishing, Inc., 2000.

Chapter 5

1, 2, 3 John
Warning Pilgrims about Dissension

Introduction

The church as a pilgrim people journeys as a community of faith. On the way, this community faces the dangers of persecution or misdirection from those outside, as we have seen in 1 Peter, 2 Peter, and Jude. But not all threats come from outside. The fabric of community can be torn by internal dissension, as the letters of John now show us.

In his commentary on the letters of John, D. Moody Smith stated: "These letters invite us to a journey of discovery, from the well known and familiar to the less familiar but nevertheless rewarding" (p. 7). As he noted, these letters call to mind many of the basic ideas of Christian faith, but they also show that living out those ideas engages the church in an ongoing struggle to define itself. Seeing how the Johannine community faced this struggle gives pilgrims of all ages guidance for their journeys of discovery.

THE SETTING OF 1, 2, 3 JOHN

THE COMPOSITION OF THE LETTERS

The letters of John, along with the Gospel of John and the book of Revelation, are all attributed by tradition to the John who was a disciple of Jesus. Only Revelation actually claims to have been written by "John," and it does not specify which John. The Gospel claims to be the testimony of one known as the "Beloved Disciple," without stating that this person was John. Both 2 and 3 John identify their author as the "Elder," but 1 John makes no claim about authorship.

The early church eventually accepted all these writings as Johannine, but it took a while. Evidence indicates that 1 John was clearly known and used in the second century and that 2 John was known by some, but 3 John does not appear in any discussions until the third century. Eusebius indicates that in the fourth century 2 and 3 John were still disputed as to authenticity. Eusebius also reports that a tradition existed about two Johns buried in Ephesus. He also cites Papias (60-130), who distinguished between the Apostle John and the Elder John.

All three letters appear to be written by the same person. Since the author of 2 and 3 John identifies himself as "the Elder," and not as an apostle, it is most likely that all three letters were composed by the person elsewhere known as the Elder John. The Gospel of John probably comes from the "Beloved Disciple," but it was obviously put in its final form by a circle of that disciple's associates (see John 21:24). All of these persons appear to have been part of the Johannine community, as it has come to be called.

The Gospel of John left its mark on the Johannine community and on the letters it produced. Raymond Brown has made a strong case for seeing the structure of that Gospel as the basic design followed in the composition of 1 John (as we will see below). The letters appear to have been composed sometime after the Gospel, thus near the very end of the first century, as attempts to correct the problems that arose from some members of the Johannine community who distorted certain ideas in the Gospel of John.

THE JOHANNINE COMMUNITY

Reading the letters of John, along with the Gospel of John and to a lesser degree the book of Revelation, reveals that they are the products of a distinctive branch of the early church. Language and concepts found in no other New Testament writings appear in those works tradition attributes to John. The letters show that this community was troubled by division and that the division was rooted in different interpretations of the community's traditions.

1 John and 2 John acknowledge this division, indicating that persons who were formerly part of the community had left. 3 John deals with the issue of one church leader refusing to recognize the leadership of the Johannine community. The first letter gives us the clearest view into the conflict. It identifies several matters of faith that lay behind the schism.

The most obvious of these had to do with views about the humanity of Christ. Readers of the Gospel of John have long recognized that the portrait of Jesus given there differs from the ones in the Synoptic Gospels. John's depiction of Jesus magnifies his glorious nature. He looms larger than life, more free of the limitations of his humanity than is true in the other Gospels. He appears as the one sent by the Father into this world of darkness to reveal the light of truth. In the second century, Gnostics, who stressed that God had given secret, saving knowledge through Jesus, used John's Gospel to support their ideas. The problem faced by the Johannine letters, though, was not Gnosticism, but rather Docetism. Docetism, a view that discounted the humanity of Jesus. Jesus only appeared or "seemed" to be human. (Docetism comes from the Greek word *dokeō*, which means "to seem.") The faction that had left the community apparently expanded on the view of Jesus given in John's Gospel and transformed Jesus into a heavenly being who visited the earth but did not really partake of human nature. The author of 1 John attacked this view and called the church back to an affirmation of the fully human incarnation of Jesus.

The opponents also apparently believed that there was no second coming of Jesus. John's Gospel downplays the second coming and focuses on the present experience of salvation. The faction expanded this idea to the point of claiming that the second coming and the future resurrection of believers were already being experienced in their lives through the indwelling of the Spirit. They carried this notion even further in asserting that they had already achieved the glorified state of sinlessness. They saw no need for a future resurrection, nor did they need to confess their sins and seek forgiveness. The author of 1 John countered that the future resurrection and final judgment of God were real and that confession of sin was still necessary.

Both 1 and 2 John indict the opponents for failing to show love. They charge the dissenters with ignoring Jesus' commandment to love one another. Their departure from the love commandment of Christ had led them into disobedience and serious misbehavior, especially in their failure to care for fellow pilgrims in need. The author of 1 John labels such persons "Antichrists," giving us the only appearance of this term in Scripture.

The Johannine community, then, was divided over basic understandings of who Christ was and what it meant to be Christian. In response to what was perceived as distortions of the Johannine traditions and rejection of the community's leaders, the letters were written to draw members back to certain basic ideas in the hope of strengthening the bonds of love.

THE MESSAGES OF 1, 2, 3 JOHN

THE STRUCTURES OF THE LETTERS

1 John

Unlike 2 and 3 John, 1 John has none of the features of a letter. Instead, it resembles a tract or treatise designed to persuade the readers to believe and do certain things. The book does not appear to be a sermon, like Hebrews, for the author repeatedly stated that he was writing to his recipients. The organization of the work is complex, making it difficult to outline. It has no logical progression of thought, but instead takes several themes and weaves them together in a swirling fashion. This swirling pattern is reminiscent of the speeches of Jesus in John's Gospel.

The basic organization of the Gospel of John also seems to be reflected in the structure of 1 John. Raymond Brown has shown that the Prologue of John's Gospel (1:1-18) is paralleled in the opening of 1 John (1:1-4) and that the twofold division of the Gospel into the Book of the Signs (John 1:19–12:50) and the Book of the Passion (13:1–20:29) is matched by the two parts of 1 John (1:5–3:10 and 3:11–5:12). The first part of the Gospel focuses on the ministry of Jesus and the opposition he encountered from "the Jews." The first part of 1 John calls the readers to walk in the light as Jesus did and deals with the opposition of those who had departed. The second part of the Gospel describes Jesus' death and his caring for his disciples, including his commandment that they love one another. The second part of 1 John gives major attention to how the community should live out this love commandment. The Gospel ends with a statement of purpose (20:30-31) and an epilogue that contains Jesus' final words to his disciples, including his instruction to "Feed my sheep" (21). 1 John ends with a statement of purpose (5:13) and a concluding thought about caring for one another and trusting in their life in Christ (5:14-21). Apart from these large divisions, the design of 1 John is not easily seen. Nonetheless, the following outline is given as a guide.

Prologue: What Was from the Beginning (1:1-4)
The Message Heard from the Beginning: God is Light (1:5–3:10)
    Living in the Light (1:5–2:2)
    Living according to His Commandment (2:3-14)
    Living in Conflict (2:15-27)
    Living in Him (2:28–3:3)
    Living against Sin (3:4-10)
The Message Heard from the Beginning: God is Love (3:11–5:12)
    Living in Love (3:11-24)
    Living in Truth (4:1-6)
    Living in True Love (4:7-21)
    Living in Victory over the World (5:1-12)
Epilogue: What Lies Ahead (5:13-21)

2 John

Both 2 and 3 John follow the typical pattern of ancient letters and are about the size of one side of a sheet of papyrus in length. Both identify the sender as the Elder. The content is very straightforward in both with little to confuse.

Prescript (1-3)
Letter Body (4-12)
    Walking in the Truth (4-6)
    Warning against Falsehood (7-11)
Close (12-13)

3 John

While apparently written by the same Elder who penned 2 John, 3 John is a personal correspondence with one person, primarily about the problems caused by another person. The prescript is briefer than is normal in letters.

Prescript (1)
Letter Body (2-12)
    Prayer and Advice for Gaius (2-8)
    The Problem of Diotrephes (9-10)
    The Testimony of Demetrius (11-12)
Close (13-15)

A SYNOPSIS OF THE THEMES

1 John

The work begins with a prologue that resembles the prologue of John's Gospel. It affirms the full incarnation of Jesus as the word of God. In the first part of the letter, the author discusses the implications of living according to the light given by God. This life requires confessing sin and seeking forgiveness. Above all, this life requires obedience to Jesus' commandment to love one another. Such obedience involves conflict with the world and with those within the church who deny the humanity of Christ. The faithful will abide in Christ and know the assurance of being God's children. Those who abide in him will oppose the lawlessness of sin.

The message of the first part is repeated somewhat with more focus on what practicing love in the community involves. Abiding in the love of God requires tangible deeds. Such acts of love show that believers are practicing the truth of God. Those who oppose the truth of God are themselves to be opposed. Their denial of the humanity of Christ and his love commandment reveals them to be antichrists. God reveals what true love is, and the faithful will demonstrate this kind of love in their lives. Those who live according to this love will experience victory over the world.

The author concludes with a recapitulation of the importance of showing true, tangible love and a word of assurance about those who abide in God.

2 John

This letter is addressed to an unnamed church commending them for the good behavior of some members but urging that love be practiced by all. The author warns the church about deceivers and instructs the church to withhold hospitality from them.

3 John

This letter is addressed to Gaius, who was apparently a church leader. Another church leader, Diotrephes, did not show proper hospitality to other Christians and rejected the Elder's authority. In contrast to his abstinence, the author commends the good example of Demetrius.

Commentary: 1 John

PROLOGUE: WHAT WAS FROM THE BEGINNING
(1:1-4)

John's "letter" begins without any epistolary formalities, revealing that this writing is not really a letter. Instead, we have a prologue that is very reminiscent of the beginning of John's Gospel. The Gospel prologue evokes the images of the creation account in Genesis 1 as it describes the coming of the eternal word (*logos*) into the world to bring God's light and life. The prologue in 1 John presupposes an awareness of John's Gospel on the part of the readers. The author stresses the reality of the word (*logos*) coming into the world: we heard it, we saw it, we touched it. This word (Christ) was life; he not only brought life, but he was and is life. This message is being declared so that the readers can share fully in the life that is Christ. Believing this message of the tangible, touchable incarnation of the word of life in Christ makes fellowship possible. As we shall see, denying it prevents fellowship.

THE MESSAGE HEARD FROM THE BEGINNING
GOD IS LIGHT
(1:5–3:10)

LIVING IN THE LIGHT
(1:5–2:2)

The first part of 1 John begins with an affirmation of God as light. The image of light is also drawn from the prologue in John's Gospel. The contrast between light and darkness was an important symbol for this community. It reflected the dualistic perspective that understood everything to be divided into one of two spheres, light and darkness. In one sphere, headed by God, one could find life, Christ, spirit, hope, forgiveness, fellowship, righteousness, and truth. In the other, headed by the evil one, one could find death, antichrist, the world, futility, guilt, exclusion, lawlessness, and falsehood. One cannot straddle the line between the two spheres. If one claims to be in the sphere of light, then there can be no sign of darkness in them, just as there is no hint of darkness in God. Those who confess to be in the light but walk in darkness live a lie. Claiming to be sinless, as the opponents were apparently doing, is to lie and miss the opportunity for forgiveness. The author does not want the readers to sin, but he accepts that they may. Like the opponents, he values perfectionism in the Christian life. But unlike them, he is aware of the pitfalls Christians face. He will not claim, as they have, to have arrived at a perfect, sinless state. Nevertheless, he does not despair, nor should the readers. God will forgive sin when it is confessed.

LIVING ACCORDING TO HIS COMMANDMENT
(2:3-14)

True knowledge of the God of light is to be found in the one who obeys God's commandments. The love of God is perfected in such a person, meaning it has attained its goal. What God's love set out to do in Christ has been achieved in the person who seeks to be obedient to God. This obedience means walking as Christ walked. How he walked is best spelled out in the new commandment Christ gave to love one another. This new commandment is not new in that it has been the mind and expression of God since the beginning. It is new, however, in that it was first explicitly given by Christ. The coming of this new commandment in Christ's word is a signal that the sphere of darkness is passing away. One cannot really live in the sphere of light if love is not actualized in their life. As true light has no room for darkness in it, true love has no room for hate in it. One cannot be in the light and hate another person. The age-old connection between being right with God and being right with other persons is stated here in a new way.

The author concludes this section in poetic fashion (1:12-14). The pair of triple expressions ("I am writing to you . . . children, fathers, young people; " "I write to you . . . children, fathers, young people") contrasts what the faithful possess from God (forgiveness, knowledge, victory) with the evil one who rules the sphere of darkness and holds his followers captive.

LIVING IN CONFLICT
(2:15-27)

Living in the light of God will necessarily involve the faithful in conflict with the sphere of darkness. They cannot love God and love the world because the two are incompatible. The world is part of the dark sphere and is passing away.

Likewise, the children of light will be in conflict with the children of darkness. The apocalyptic message the readers were familiar with contained a prediction of the coming of some kind of antichrist. The term here does not appear to mean a particular person, as it later came to mean. Instead, the writer considers this antichrist prediction to have been fulfilled already in the form of those who departed from the community. They belong to the sphere of darkness, and always have. If they had truly been in the sphere of light, they would not have returned to the darkness. The fact that they went out from them proves to the author that they never were truly part of the community.

What was their great sin that led to their expulsion or withdrawal from the Johannine community? The author indicates that they had denied that Jesus is the Christ (2:22). In 4:2 their erroneous position becomes clearer. They were not denying the deity of Christ nor that he is the way to salvation. They were denying that the divine Christ was actually the man Jesus. They held either that the Christ only appeared to be the man Jesus or that the divine Christ had occupied the body of the man Jesus for a while. They could not accept that the true Son of God from the spiritual world could become material human flesh. As the author has argued that the God of light cannot contain darkness, they would have argued that the God who is spirit (see John 4:24) cannot contain evil matter.

The author has written to expose the error of the dissenters. Yet, because this is the Johannine community that placed a heavy emphasis on the Paraclete promised by Jesus as their guide into all truth, the writer also affirms that they already have it within themselves to know the truth. They have received the anointing from God that will guide them. Nonetheless, he does write because even those who possess the Paraclete can benefit from a human word. Later, he acknowledges that not everyone who claims to possess the spirit actually does (4:1).

LIVING IN HIM
(2:28–3:3)

The anointing they have received as God's children has taught them to abide in "him." Whether the him is God or Christ is not always clear, but generally it seems to refer to Christ. Their identity as "children" of

God is stressed. The term implies relationship, but it also suggests more. It has to do with being "begotten" by God. They have been born from above into the sphere of light. Those who have not been so begotten do not know the truth. Hence, the world did not know who Christ really was when he came. This is another important theme in the Fourth Gospel, that those to whom Jesus came did not recognize him. Darkness cannot "comprehend" the light. But the children of light can; they can already see. What the author assures them of, however, is that there is more yet to see. They have seen Christ, but when he comes again, they will see themselves in an even newer light: they will be like him.

LIVING AGAINST SIN
(3:4-10)

In the meantime they must struggle against the lawlessness of sin. Lawlessness is a typical characterization of sin in apocalyptic writing. It refers not to civil disobedience but to defiance of God's rule. The world of darkness opposes the sovereignty of God. All humans were born into this world of lawlessness, but God has forgiven the faithful and birthed them into a new world. As children of this new world, they cannot continue to commit sin. Previously, the author acknowledged that true believers can sin, and be forgiven. Here, however, he is urging them not to presume upon this forgiveness. To commit sin is to betray that one is really a child of the devil.

How can the writer have it both ways? Can Christians sin or not? He seems to say yes on the one hand and no on the other. Reference to Greek verb tenses and grammar, though often tried, offers no legitimate resolution of this issue. There is ambiguity. When the author is attacking those who claim to have achieved perfection, he accuses them of calling God a liar. When addressing those who might be tempted to rely too easily on God's forgiveness, he warns them that sinning is incompatible with true Christian living. We have a writer addressing different concerns, not a systematic theologian trying to define a doctrine of sin. The thrust of his message here is that pilgrims cannot grow lazy on the journey. The Lord who is coming is expecting to find the children behaving.

THE MESSAGE HEARD FROM THE BEGINNING
GOD IS LOVE
(3:11–5:12)

LIVING IN LOVE
(3:11-24)

The second part of the book seems to begin at 3:11. Once again the author refers to "the message you have heard from the beginning." This phrase, appearing here and back at 1:5, recalls the opening verse (1:1) and takes the writing in a slightly different direction. Most of the themes included earlier are repeated, but the orientation becomes more slanted toward life in the community.

The section begins with a reaffirmation of the love commandment. Cain stands as the supreme example of one who let his hatred for his brother take him outside the grace of God. The faithful should expect the same hatred from the world. Hatred is a part of the sphere of darkness; it is one of the strongest weapons in the realm of death. In contrast, love is the operative force in the sphere of light. That is so because love is of God, clearly evidenced in God's own experience of the hatred of this world in the death of God's son. That death, brought on by love, compels the Christian to love, even to the point of death. But it also compels loving short of death, as for example when a brother or sister has need of the world's goods. Love need not always be heroic as in martyrdom; love compels responding to the most basic human needs.

It is this love in action that gives the children of God assurance before God. Even if they have doubts about their standing before God stemming from their own heart (we would say conscience), the truth of love in action can assure believers that they are doing what God requires. This requirement is repeated: that we love one another (3:23). Keeping this commandment is the only assurance Christians need. It is testimony that they abide in God and God abides in them. They have the further assurance, however, of the Spirit.

LIVING IN TRUTH
(4:1-6)

But spirits have to be tested. As in the Old Testament, where everyone who claimed to have the spirit of God did not always speak truthfully, not everyone who claims the Spirit's guidance delivers a truthful word. Here, the author gives us a clue about early Christian prophetic preaching. As was the case in Paul's exchanges with the Corinthians, persons in the community could become empowered by the Spirit to speak a word from the Lord. For the Corinthians, steeped in Greek traditions of ecstatic divination, trancelike pronouncements were considered to be a sign of the message's authenticity. The community of "John" knows similar ecstatic pronouncements. Such messages have to be evaluated, however, the author asserts. No one can really be in the Spirit of God and say that Jesus is not from God. Apparently some of those denying the humanity of Christ had expressed their conviction through spirit-preaching. The words themselves have to be judged, our author argues, as they did in the Old Testament cases. Only those affirming that "Christ has come *in the flesh*" are true spiritual messengers of God.

LIVING IN TRUE LOVE
(4:7-21)

The writer returns to the necessity of love for the community. Spirit-speaking aside, those in whom God's Spirit abides will be engaged in loving action. This is true love. This is the truth God revealed in sending the Son to die, and this is the truth that will distinguish the true follower from the false. This is how God is revealed to the community, in its acts of love. The author then repeats much that he has already written, stressing that the true test of whether or not one abides in God and has assurance before God is whether or not they show true love. One cannot truly love the invisible God if one cannot love the clearly visible fellow human.

LIVING IN VICTORY OVER THE WORLD
(5:1-12)

Those who confess that Jesus (the real human man) is the Christ and who live in love are born of God in victory over the world. This basic confession of faith is the sure sign that the world has been conquered. God has given a sure sign of divine love in the incarnation, the real, flesh-and-blood embodiment of Jesus.

This Jesus came by water and blood, both of which witness to the truth of the message heard from the beginning. To the water and blood is joined a third witness: the Spirit. The witness of the Spirit is fairly clear, but exactly what is meant by water and blood is unclear. Generally, two routes to understanding these "elements" are taken. Either the water and blood refer to the story of the incarnated Jesus or they are to be taken sacramentally as references to baptism and the Eucharist. If they refer to Jesus, it is clear that the blood is to be associated with his crucifixion. The water, however, could mean the water of human birth, the water of Jesus' own baptism by John, or the water that flowed from Jesus' side on the cross (according to John). Water birth and cross blood both affirm the point of the fully human

incarnation that has been of concern throughout. Water baptism and
the blood of crucifixion might actually be distorted into support for
the opponents since they may have been the type of Docetists who
held that the Christ spirit descended on the man Jesus at baptism and
left him when he died on the cross. The flow of water and blood from
the cross would more clearly parallel the Gospel of John's crucifixion
scene.

One cannot automatically dismiss the sacramental interpretation.
John's Gospel strangely has no Lord's Supper in it, and its account of
the baptism by John differs from the Synoptics. Some take this to
mean that the Johannine community was nonsacramental or anti-
sacramental and did not observe baptism and the Eucharist. Others
see symbolic references to both sacraments in the Gospel. Since 1 John
speaks of the water and blood as continuing witnesses, some would
also see a reference here to the sacraments.

Ultimately, even if the sacraments are intended, even they are
viewed as witnesses themselves to the death of Christ. This triple-
attested testimony from God should certainly surpass the tests
whereby human testimony is accepted, the author says. The final
testimony is the life we have in Christ.

EPILOGUE: WHAT LIES AHEAD
(5:13-21)

The author ends with a statement of purpose: that the readers might
have eternal life. This statement of purpose matches the expressed
purpose of the Gospel of John (20:31). The rest of the letter is a
rephrasing of the ideas already covered; thus it constitutes a recapitulation. The focus here, though, is not so much on "the message heard
from the beginning" as it is on what remains to be done. Christians are
to live boldly, trusting in God. They are to watch after fellow members
of the community, interceding before God on their behalf. They are to
trust their identity as God's children as they strive to overcome sin
and the evil one. Above all, they are to trust that they posses the truth
who Jesus Christ is, the word of eternal life.

Commentary: 2 John

PRESCRIPT
(1-3)

The letter begins with a simple identification of the sender as "The
Elder." As noted above, tradition has identified this elder as John the
Apostle. The fact that he does not call himself apostle is an argument

against the tradition. If connected with a John at all, the link is then most likely to that Elder John Papias referred to in the portion of his writing preserved by Eusebius. Why he would have been known as the Elder when many other persons held the position of elder in the early church is unknown. It conceivably could have risen from a deliberate effort within the Johannine community to distinguish between the apostle John and the "elder" John.

The author writes authoritatively to the elect lady and her children. In all likelihood, this is a symbolic term for the church and its members. The fact that no specific place is named suggests that the letter was intended for more than one church under the guidance of the Elder. The recipients' identity is elaborated upon to indicate up front something of the concern of the letter. The Elder loves the lady in the truth, and affirms that this love is shared by all who abide in the truth.

The greeting resembles the greetings of Paul, except that the word mercy is added (as in the Pastoral Epistles). Grace (*charis*) is an expansion of the stock Greek greeting *chairein* (greeting!), and peace is the Greek equivalent of the Hebrew *shalom*. Typical Johannine terms are added at the end: truth and love.

LETTER BODY
(4-12)

WALKING IN THE TRUTH
(4-6)

The body of the letter begins with a positive affirmation that some of the members are known to the Elder to be walking in the truth. A subtle inference easily drawn is that he also knows that some were not. The author then states his main point: let us all live according to the love commandment. The language is very similar to 1 John and establishes a clear link between the two. In fact, verses 4-6 state succinctly the main thrust of 1 John.

WARNING AGAINST FALSEHOOD
(7-11)

Another concern has also occasioned this letter. Walking in truth requires walking away from falsehood. "Many deceivers have gone out into the world." The way the Elder says that these deceivers have gone out suggests that he has in mind the same dissenters spoken against in 1 John. They were persons who had left the Johannine community. The Elder is warning the elect lady about them. As in 1 John, they are called *antichrist*. They are dangerous in that they can lead people astray. Such persons should not be tolerated; in fact, the hospitality that was normally required of churches is to be withheld from them. To welcome them is to participate in their evil. Love for one another apparently does not include the deceivers.

CLOSE
(12-13)

The close of 2 John has two parts. In the first the author indicates that he has much more to say about these matters but prefers to do it in person. In antiquity, letters were considered to be substitutes for personal visits. The fact that the Elder can refrain from writing more suggests that he anticipated being able to make such a visit soon.

The second part of the close gives a greeting from the church of the Elder.

Commentary: 3 John

PRESCRIPT
(1)

The opening of 3 John closely resembles that of 2 John. The name of the sender is stated simply. Unlike 2 John, though, this letter is addressed to one individual, Gaius, about whom we know nothing else. From the body of the letter, it appears that Gaius was a leader, if not the pastor, of a church. Gaius is called beloved, a favorite Johannine term. He is called beloved three more times below. He is loved "in truth," also Johannine language. The letter opening does not include the typical greeting.

LETTER BODY
(2-12)

PRAYER AND ADVICE FOR GAIUS
(2-8)

Verse 2 resembles somewhat the prayer section that is often found in letters. The Elder knows the good condition of Gaius' inner self, and he hopes that all will go well for the outer self, too. The Elder has heard a good word about Gaius, and he commends him on his faithfulness to the truth. As 1 John makes clear, walking in the truth means showing love to brothers and sisters. Gaius has done that. The Elder's hope, and one reason for writing the letter, is that Gaius' love for the "friends" who have stopped by his church and enjoyed his hospitality will extend to sending them on with additional support. In a sense, the letter is a recommendation of these friends and a solicitation of support (probably monetary) for their ministry.

THE PROBLEM OF DIOTREPHES
(9-10)

Another motive also lies behind this letter. Diotrephes has become a problem. The Elder indicates that Diotrophes has refused to acknowledge the Elder's authority. Since the Elder says he had written to the church, it seems likely that Diotrephes was the leader of the same church as Gaius. The Elder is thus writing to another person in the church, Gaius, to report what Diotrephes had done. Unlike Gaius, Diotrephes had not received the persons sent from the Elder. Furthermore, he had kept others from receiving it, too. The Elder castigates Diotrephes as evil and promises to address this matter in person.

In all of this we see something of a power struggle in the early church. We have no reason to connect Diotrephes to the dissenters opposed in 1 John, that is, unless 3 John was written before 1 John. What appears to have been happening was a local resistance to the authority of one church and its leaders over another. Doctrinal issues may have been the cause, but we are not told that.

THE TESTIMONY OF DEMETRIUS
(11-12)

In contrast to the evil example of Diotrephes, Gaius should observe the model behavior of Demetrius, whose identity is otherwise unclear. Demetrius may have been another leader in the church, or he may have been one of the persons Diotrephes refused to receive. If so, then he may also have been one of those friends to whom Gaius had extended hospitality. Thus, the letter would again function as a recommendation for Demetrius and the other friends.

CLOSE
(13-15)

3 John ends much as 2 John with a statement about hoping to visit soon and an extension of greetings from other friends.

FOR FURTHER READING

Brown, Raymond E. *The Epistles of John.* Anchor Bible 30. New York: Doubleday, 1982.

_____. *The Community of the Beloved Disciple.* New York: Paulist Press, 1979.

Culpepper, R. Alan. "Gospel and Letters of John." *Mercer Dictionary of the Bible.* Macon GA: Mercer University Press, 1990.

Marshall, I. Howard. *The Epistles of John.* New International Commentary on the New Testament. Grand Rapids: Wm. B. Eerdmans Publishing Co., 1978.

Polhill, John B. "First, Second, and Third John." *Mercer Commentary on the Bible.* Macon GA: Mercer University Press, 1995.

Smalley, Stephen S. *1, 2, 3 John.* Word Biblical Commentary. Waco TX: Word Books, 1984.

Smith, D. Moody. *First, Second, and Third John.* Interpretation. Louisville KY: John Knox Press, 1991.

Chapter 6

Revelation
The Destination of Pilgrims

Introduction

As with the other New Testament writings examined in this book, Revelation deals with the theme of pilgrimage. More pointedly than the other books, however, Revelation offers a vision of the destination of pilgrims. As in Hebrews, Revelation sometimes likens the church to those ancient Israelites, liberated by the Exodus and journeying from slavery toward the promised land. Exodus imagery is abundant in Revelation, especially in the way John's depictions of the woes that befall the rebellious earth resemble the Exodus story of the plagues on stubborn Egypt.

The way toward the heavenly destination is fraught with danger for pilgrims, both as temptation and tribulation. The faithful pilgrim, though, is encouraged to persevere by the assurance that what happens is a working out of the will of God and by the glorious vision of what life lived under the lordship of God, with all the forces of evil finally subdued, is like. Faithful pilgrims do not give up or give in; they keep moving forward, even into the darkness of death, confident that the one who came as the lamb of sacrifice has in his death already sealed the fate of those forces opposed to God and of those persons who are faithful.

THE LAST BOOK OF THE BIBLE

The book of Revelation is the last book in the Bible. Not everyone has welcomed its inclusion in the canon of Christian scriptures warmly. Much of its history has been marked by controversy. In fact, since one of the reasons it seems to have been written was to oppose certain views that had developed in those churches in eastern Asia Minor to which it was first addressed, we can safely assume that not everyone in those churches accepted its message even then.

Revelation was gradually accepted by a large number of early Christians, however, and within a few decades was used widely, and not only in Asia Minor. Evidence indicates that Christians in Egypt, North Africa, Rome, and Gaul had come to use it at least by the early years of the third century. Because certain heretical groups used it a lot in the late second century, many Christians looked upon it with suspicion. As late as the early fourth century, Eusebius of Caesarea in Palestine indicated that it was still much disputed as to its inclusion in the emerging canon of New Testament scriptures. The churches in the East especially had difficulty accepting it; the eastern branch of the Syrian church never did. Even after it became firmly established as a part of the Bible for most Christians, many of them still avoided it. The Protestant reformers of the sixteenth century expressed many reservations about the book of Revelation. Understandably, many readers today avoid the book, either because they find its imagery enigmatic and troubling or because they are troubled by the many bizarre interpretations that are currently popular.

Yet Revelation is there in the canon as the last book of the Bible. Of course, it was not written as the last book of the Bible. Revelation was written originally for the seven congregations it names in chapters 2 and 3. It was sent to them not as a book, that is, as a public document intended for general reading, but as a letter, that is, as a message intended for a specific people in a specific time.

But why the form of a letter? One reason may be that about the time Revelation was probably written a collection of the letters of Paul had come to be preserved and used by some churches, especially churches in Asia Minor. If so, then a pattern had been set. The voice of the apostles could be heard in their letters. As was originally the case with Paul's letters, Revelation was intended to be a written substitute for the author's presence to the people with whom he intended to communicate. The first recipients of Revelation would have read it or heard it as a message from John intended for them.

REVELATION'S FIRST READERS

Who were those original recipients? They were Christians living in seven cities in eastern Asia Minor. Revelation was probably aimed not just at the Christians in those particular cities but also at those in the other cities and towns of the region. Christianity had been established there in the 50s by Paul and his co-workers. In the period after the Jewish war with Rome (70s), a large number of Jews and Jewish-Christian immigrants flooded into this area. Jews were struggling with the issues of determining who they were going to be after the destruction of the temple and many of those other institutions that had been the basis for their life as a people.

Jewish Christians were also dealing with such issues, but were going in a different direction. Many Christians saw themselves as the true Israel, which now included gentiles as well as Jewish followers of Jesus the Christ. The different struggles of non-Christian Jews and Christians (both Jewish and gentile) often led to conflict between them. The Jews still enjoyed some of the special privileges granted to them by the Roman government, for example, exemption from military service and from paying homage to Caesar. Jews were expected to pray for Caesar, but not to him. Other people were expected to pray to Caesar as to a god.

For Christians, this presented a dilemma. When their separation from Judaism became more obvious, they no longer could benefit from the special status of Jews. They were members of a suspect religion that seemed to be unpatriotic and irreligious. Thus, they were subject to social and economic discrimination, expressed through constant tension and frequent harassment. Unofficial persecution by mob violence was also a real possibility.

The earliest tradition about Revelation, that of Irenaeus in the late second century, places the book near the end of Domitian's reign (81–96), thus in the early 90s. Some modern scholars prefer dating it earlier to the time of Claudius (41–54) or Nero (54–68) and a few to as late as Trajan (98–117), but most opt for around 95 at the end of Domitian's reign. This is due partly to Irenaeus' view and partly to the apparent use of Babylon as a code name for Rome. Other writings refer to Rome this way, but this seems to have happened only after the Romans destroyed the Jewish temple in A.D. 70, just as the Babylonians had destroyed the temple of Solomon in 586 B.C.

These were difficult times for the eastern Roman empire, due to the threat of the Parthians, famine, earthquakes, and internal disorder. It was also a difficult time for Christians. Deciding what it meant to be a follower of Jesus and a member of the true Israel were vital issues. The book of Revelation indicates that Christians should expect immediate problems with the governmental leaders, resulting in persecution. The author expressed his view that the first signs of this impending persecution were already evident. A full-scale persecution sponsored by the Roman government did not break out until much later, but the threat of such persecution was real and a reason for alarm. Christians led a precarious existence. The focal point was the emperor cult, which was prominent in Asia Minor. Would the Christians accept the claims that the emperor was Lord and God, or would they hold firmly to their conviction that only Jesus was Lord?

Eugene Boring has identified six basic options that presented themselves to the Christians in Asia Minor (Boring, 21-23). (1) They could quit being Christians. (2) They could lie about being Christians. (3) They could take up arms to defend themselves. (4) They could change the law. (5) They could accommodate their faith and accept certain pagan elements. (6) They could remain faithful even unto death. Options 1 and 2 were the easiest paths but meant betrayal of the faith. Options 3 and 4 were not realistic. Option 5 presented itself to many as an acceptable, reasonable alternative in the face of danger. Revelation advocates only option 6 and sharply rebukes anyone for taking any other option.

A DIFFERENT KIND OF BOOK

Although written as a letter, the author of Revelation calls his work a prophecy (1:3; 19:10; 22:7-10, 18-19). As a prophecy, the work stood in the long tradition of Hebrew prophetic works that were seen as the messages of God to chosen servants who conveyed to the people what God had revealed. These prophetic messages had been interpretations of the prophets' own circumstances, with clear calls to faithfulness to God in the face of trial. Jews, and also early Christians, believed that Hebrew prophecy had come to an end with the last books of the Hebrew Bible (Old Testament) but also that in the last days God would again raise up prophets. Revelation is clearly intended to be seen this way. One indication of this is the way Revelation uses Old Testament prophetic passages and reinterprets them for its own time. The book is almost a mosaic of Old Testament prophetic works woven into a new tapestry indicating God's action in the present and near future.

Revelation calls itself a work of prophecy; it follows the basic pattern of a letter. As for substance, however, both in terms of concepts and language, Revelation is an example of "apocalyptic" writing. Apocalyptic writings flourished among Jews from about 200 B.C. to just after A.D. 100. They typically contained imaginative visions of another world or of the future that were intended to give hope to people living in a world that stood powerfully opposed to the Jewish understanding of God and godly living.

Early Christians were deeply influenced by apocalyptic ideas and sometimes used the vehicle of apocalyptic writing to express their view of faith and faithfulness. The ideas, images, perspectives, and approach to Old Testament scriptures that we see in other apocalyptic works are abundant in Revelation. In fact, the author states that this work of prophecy sent as a letter to seven churches is the apocalypse (revelation) of Jesus Christ (1:1).

As apocalyptic, Revelation's language is more pictorial than propositional. Boring has given a detailed comparison of pictorial and propositional modes of expression (51-59). Propositional language tries to operate by logic; everything must be sequential and rational. It also is diachronic, that is, dealing with things one at a time in chronological order. It is also objectifying, understanding that everything it talks about has a referent in the real world. Even symbols have to have an actual referent. Such language also draws a contrast between truth and myth, taking myth to refer to something that is not real or true.

Apocalyptic language, on the other hand, is more pictorial. It does not logically and diachronically articulate a system of doctrine. It uses symbols to paint a picture. It cannot point immediately to a referent in the real world because it is describing realities that are beyond the so-called real world. It intends to convey a feeling or a sense of what that other world is like, recognizing that it cannot be completely expressed in propositional language. Its symbols are not tied to a one-for-one correspondence to any earthly entity. Such language is called *polyvalent*, meaning it is capable of referring to any number of referents. It uses such language to say what certain earthly realities are like in a larger perspective. The particular entities identified by the author are not the only things that the symbols can signify. Anything that fits the picture can be a legitimate referent. Thus, it can draw on symbolic, mythic images to convey the true nature of such entities. It can use the language of myth to convey truth, ultimate truth, which is always true.

READING REVELATION

Several ways of trying to understand the language and imagery of Revelation have been followed by interpreters. (1) Some read it as non-historical (spiritual), as not having any particular connection to historical referents. It was intended to deal with timeless truths. (2) Some read it as church-historical language (continuous historical), that is, that it was intended to give a history of the church for however long the church would last or for particular periods in the life of the church. (3) Some read it as end-historical (futurist), that is, that it only speaks to a future period when all of the things it talks about will begin to happen. (4) Some take it as contemporary-historical (preterist), referring only to the events encountered by the church of John's day. This view holds that any interpretation of Revelation must take seriously what the writing meant for its original readers.

The approach to Revelation followed here draws from most of these other approaches. We begin by assuming that the author, John, had an urgent message from God to deliver to his readers. He had something to communicate that was relevant and meaningful for them. He did not produce a work that would only have relevance at some distant, future time. His readers would not have found much comfort in being told that far down the road, say some time in the early twenty-first century, all that he was describing to them would come to pass. If that had been John's goal, it is doubtful that the book of Revelation would have survived. Who would have bothered reading it? Who would have heard a word from God for them in it? Who would have risked their lives to preserve its message? No, the first readers of Revelation believed that John had sent them a message from God that was relevant for their time and place. They would have tried to find meaning in his cryptic symbols that made sense for them. They would have believed that he was talking about their own experience, and they would have been correct. He was describing their experience.

But John was doing more than just describing their experience. He was explaining the meaning of their experience. To do that he had to probe beneath the surface of what was happening and explore the deeper dimensions of what was going on in their time and place. When he did, John understood that the surface realities that made up their own experience were momentary expressions of deeper, greater realities. He looked at what was happening in his world at that time, and he understood the truth about it because he could sense, in true prophetic fashion, the real forces at work. He did not look beyond their experience; he peered deep into its innermost dimensions and saw what was really there. In doing so, John tapped the vein of ultimate realities. He saw what was true, what had always been true, and what would always be true. He read his own time in the light of eternity, in the light of God.

To communicate what he saw, John relied on pictorial language, the language of metaphor and myth. He could not do otherwise and effectively communicate the grandeur and glory of what he saw. Simple, logical, propositional language was inadequate. It always is when we are really dealing with the things of God. Such language imposes frail human ways of thinking on that which defies full comprehension. John refused to try to reduce his vision of God and God's ways to an organized system of theological doctrine. Such systems of thought may serve us well at times as we try to communicate with each other about God, but they can never adequately express the full reality of God. John opted to depict his vision in imagery that transcended the normal human ways of seeing. That way, his readers could also see something of what he had seen, something that was ultimately beyond description but could be pointed to in powerful symbols.

The effectiveness of John's vivid imagery partly explains the history of the interpretation of the book of Revelation. In almost every generation of Christians since the time John wrote, there have been interpreters who were convinced John was describing their own time and place. They have seen in the symbols of his book clear allusions to what they believed was happening or was going to happen soon. Thus, they have concluded that John was talking about their time, and only their time. They have matched particular images in Revelation with persons, institutions, and events of their time and have believed that

John was "predicting" that all these things would happen. They have also often joined John's images with other passages from the Bible in order to fashion a calendar so that they could predict when everything John described would occur. Such interpretations have become so popular in our own time that many people, if not most, naturally assume that this way of reading John's book is the only way to do so.

Of course, such interpreters are wrong, in a sense. Every interpretation of Revelation that has used the book to construct a scenario of the end of time has been proven wrong. Every interpretation that has understood that John intended to describe and predict the events of their own time or of some moment in the near future has outlived its usefulness. Time has marched on, and such predictive interpretations have been left in the dust. Such interpretations have failed not so much because the interpreters have constructed a flawed timetable but because such interpretations misunderstand the whole intention of Revelation. John was not predicting events in the distant future; he was describing his own time. Interpretation must begin with the understanding that John had a relevant message for the Christians of eastern Asia Minor in the first century.

In a sense, however, those who have seen John speaking about their own time and place have been correct, though their attempts to restrict John's message to the events of their own experience have been erroneous. John tapped the deep veins of true reality in his own time so well that he brought to light certain forces that are operative in all times and places. No wonder readers have thought he was speaking directly to them! No wonder they could identify parts of their own experience in the wild images of his visions! Though John's vision was focused on his own time, he described the truth of his own time in such a way that his message is true for all times.

Those who would limit the interpretation of Revelation to decoding his symbols and discovering how they relate to matters in John's time also miss the significance of John's accomplishment. He peered deep into the events of his day and saw what was really happening, not just what appeared on the surface. What he saw through the events of his time is still true. The struggle between good and evil, between God and the forces of evil, between the people of God and the earthly manifestations of evil, though manifested in John's time in the church and the Roman empire, are manifested in other times in other ways. Guided by John's illuminating vision, when we peer deeply into our own experience, we can see that sometimes we are the faithful ones striving to contend with the claims of the great Beast. Sometimes, however, even in our churches, we find ourselves on the side of demonic oppression. When we see beyond the surface, beyond the temporary instances of this struggle in our own time, and perceive, as

John did, what is really going on in the world and in us, then we, too, have seen and heard the enduring message of John's great book.

THE MESSAGE OF REVELATION

THE STRUCTURE THE BOOK

As we have already noted, John Bunyan entitled his famous allegorical work on the Christian life, *The Pilgrim's Progress from This World to That Which Is to Come.* His extended title continues: *Delivered under the Similitude of a Dream wherein Is Discovered the Manner of His Setting Out, His Dangerous Journey, and Safe Arrival at the Desired Country.* Bunyan saw that he could best depict the pilgrim's journey only in pictorial language. Thus, he called his work a *Similitude.* It was cast in the symbolic form of a dream, in which he saw the truth about Christian existence in the world being acted out. The characters and places in the symbolic dream depict real dimensions of the Christian life.

In much the same way, Revelation describes the struggles of the Christian life in vivid, sometimes bizarre, symbols. For John, these symbols came not in a dream but in a series of visions. Bunyan spoke of the Christian struggle in terms of a "setting out," a "dangerous journey," and a "safe arrival." We have already seen how the book of Hebrews focuses on the setting out and how James through Jude focus on the dangerous journey. Revelation focuses on the safe arrival. Of course, Hebrews is also aware that the life of pilgrimage is fraught with danger and that the way to the safe arrival lies along the road of faithfulness. Likewise, James through Jude recognize the importance of beginning the journey well and of keeping our eyes on the ultimate destination. Revelation focuses on the destination, but it also is mindful that there must be a good beginning of the journey toward this destination and that the way toward it is a hazardous one. In a sense, all of these books have in mind the total life of pilgrimage. Different books stress different dimensions of the same experience. Revelation stresses the importance of the good ending. Confidence in the ending inspires faithfulness along the way.

The basic pattern of the book of Revelation is similar to that found in other apocalypses. The book moves from a description of the present experience of the intended readers, to a depiction of a period of increased eschatological distress leading up to the End, to a description of the final victory of God at the arrival of the End. This pattern echoes the pattern of the Christian life. Again, we have a setting out, a dangerous journey, and a safe arrival.

Isolating the structure of the movements in the book gives us the following outline.

The Prelude (1:1-8)
 The Title (1:1-3)
 The Letter Opening (1:4-8)
First Movement: The Present Experience of Pilgrims (1:9–3:22)
 The Initial Vision (1:9-20)
 The Letters to the Seven Churches (2:1–3:22)
Second Movement: The Intensification of Troubles for Pilgrims (4:1–18:24)
 The Throne of God (4:1-11)
 The Lamb of God (5:1-14)
 The Seven Seals (6:1–8:1)
 The Seven Angels and the Seven Trumpets (8:2–11:19)
 The Struggle with Evil and Assurances of Victory (12:1–14:20)
 The Seven Angels and the Seven Plagues (15:1–16:21)
 The Fall of Babylon (17:1–18:24)
Third Movement: The Final Victory of God for Pilgrims (19:1–22:5)
 Heavenly Praise for God's Victory (19:1-10)
 Scenes of the End (19:11–22:5)
The Postlude (22:6-21)
 The Close of the Vision (22:6-17)
 John's Last Word (22:18-21)

A SYNOPSIS OF THE THEMES

Revelation begins with a description of the present troubles of John and his readers (chs. 1–3). This includes a vision of Christ, who, in his exalted state, reveals to John a message from God for the churches in seven cities in Asia Minor. The Christians in these cities are called to be faithful to God.

The book then depicts the intensification of troubles anticipated for the book's first readers and for their world (4:1–18:24). This includes a vision of the heavenly throne room where Christ, as the slaughtered-resurrected lamb, opens seven seals of a book. This leads to the sounding of seven trumpets and then to the pouring out of seven bowls of wrath. The outpouring of God's wrath culminates in the destruction of Babylon, the Great City, which receives the full judgment of God.

The last section is a description of the final victory (19:1–22:5). The climax of this victory is the appearance of the heavenly Jerusalem, the Holy City, which receives the full redemption of God. The book closes (22:6-21) with words of promise and warning.

In each of these three movements, we are told who the Actor is: in every case it is God as God is defined in Christ. God is the One who acts, but how God acts has already been revealed in the historical moment of Jesus Christ. Jesus came, preached the need for repentance, and identified with sinners and announced their forgiveness and inclusion in the kingdom; he suffered, died, and was resurrected in victory over evil and death. This is the story of Christ on earth, and it reveals the way God acts. In each of these movements we are also told specifically how God acts: God speaks, then judges, and then redeems.

Each movement begins with an opening vision of transcendence that features either the glorified Christ or God in heaven. These opening visions of God or Christ are then followed by a series of visions, with the number seven figuring prominently in the structure. Groups of seven also appear scattered throughout the book. The use of seven indicates that a complete message is being given. From beginning to end, momentum builds. Each new series of visions is more intense than the one before. The series do not represent separate phases in the scheme of history but rather provide progressively more dramatic descriptions of the conflict of forces leading to the end. When we finally reach the end, with God's triumph over evil, all heaven and earth erupt with the grateful victor's song.

Commentary

THE PRELUDE
(1:1-8)

The first major movement of Revelation is preceded by a prelude, which functions as the opening of the book. The prelude contains two parts. The first part gives John's title for the book, indicating what kind of writing it is (1:1-3). The second part is a typical letter opening, similar to the letters of Paul (1:4-8).

THE TITLE
(1:1-3)

"The revelation of Jesus Christ . . ." The work is called the *apokalypsis* (revelation) of Jesus Christ. Inherent in this word is the idea that something previously hidden is being unveiled. Grammatically this could mean a revelation "about" Jesus or a revelation "from" Jesus. Here it evidently is "from" Jesus, the exalted Lord of the church who is present with the church and speaks a prophetic word to it.

"Which God gave him . . ." But the revelation does not originate with Jesus; it comes from God. Thus, the revelation as a whole can also be called the word of God (v. 2). As in Genesis 1:1, the first verb has God as its subject: God gave. God is the actor throughout, even when God is in the background, unseen. God gave the revelation to Jesus. It is mediated through him. Jesus is the one who "testifies" (v. 2) to God. For Christians, God is known through Jesus. This Jesus is the one who was tried and killed by the Romans, the one who died for us, the one who defines who God is for us. He does not take the place of God. God is the one who acts in and through Jesus. But Jesus is the indispensable window through which we see God acting

"He made it known by sending his angel . . ." Jesus communicated the message to the churches. The verb *esēmanen* (made known) is related to the noun *sēmeion* (sign). Literally, Jesus "signified" the message. He put it in sign language. We are told up front that we are dealing with symbols, images, not straightforward words. The message points us to a reality that can only be expressed in pictures.

The message does not come directly to the churches from Jesus. It is mediated first through an angel, identified as his servant, as is John and as are the recipients of the revelation. Angels figure prominently in apocalypses, and they do so here in Revelation. But they are creatures of God, as are humans. They hold no special power over humans and are not to be worshiped, as was perhaps the case in the first century, especially in Asia Minor.

"To his servant John . . ." John is a crucial part of the process of revelation here. The words are his words, describing all that he saw. They are the word of God, but they are put in his human words, reflecting his thought patterns and his circumstances. Exactly who this John is we are not told. God calls him his "servant." He later calls himself "your brother" (1:9). He says that he shares the tribulation and the kingdom and patient endurance with his readers. He also says that he was on the island of Patmos "because" of the word of God and the testimony of Jesus, the same phrase used in verse 2. He could mean he was there because he had preached that word, or he could mean he was there in order to receive the word. Later tradition said he was John the apostle; others in the early church disagreed.

"To show his servants . . ." The last links in the revelatory chain named here are the human recipients of John's message in the churches. They also are called "servants." John's experience was not a private affair. It was to be shared. Most likely, it would be shared in a communal setting of worship, probably originally read in one sitting, as were other communications from church leaders. As servants, though, the word is not finally for them. Servants "testify" to what they have received from God. As the angel did and John did, the church members have a role in testifying about God's actions to the world.

"Blessed is/are. . . ." The title also contains a double blessing. The one reading aloud (again indicating a worship setting) and the listeners are blessed. The hearing is understood in the full biblical sense of obeying: Blessed are "those who hear and who keep what is written in it." As in the case of Old Testament blessings and Jesus' Beatitudes, the pronouncement of blessing conveys a state of blessedness. It both announces who the blessed ones are and is the vehicle for their realization of the blessing.

The revelation is about "what must soon take place." Verse 3 adds, "for the time is near." The theme of nearness is stressed throughout the book. For those first readers/hearers, the message was urgent. They were to understand that what was being described would take place soon. This is a common apocalyptic theme, one that can cause problems for the modern reader. Much that Revelation talks about did not take place soon for John's readers. In fact, much that Revelation indicates would take place has never occurred, to the disappointment of many interpreters through the ages. The question arises as to how readers should view such apparently unrealized eschatological hopes.

Some readers of Revelation and other apocalyptic passages in the New Testament consider expectations of an imminent End to be fundamentally off base. The best approach, they think, is simply to reject such notions altogether, as did the early Gnostic heretics. Such is the conclusion of modern readers who consign Revelation to the back shelf as an amusing, well-intentioned, but misguided work.

Other readers have sought some way to reinterpret such references to an imminent End. They may argue that soon did not mean soon. It actually meant later. John knew this, they say. He did not expect the End to happen in his time. He was actually writing about a distant future. Most readers who have taken this view believed that they, not John, were living in the last days. Others say end did not mean "end". It meant something else, such as the coming of the Spirit in a fuller way. In this view John was not describing an actual end; he only used such language to speak of something else.

Still other readers try to move beyond the particular time intended by John and affirm the conviction of urgency that permeates the letter. John meant the end was coming soon. It did not. But his kind of expectation is what readers need to have. For the reader of all times the end is "always" near. John's conviction of urgency can be affirmed without accepting his timetable, which was a regular part of the apocalyptic genre in which he wrote. Nearly all apocalypses, including Daniel and the shorter ones in the New Testament, contain such an expectation. Such a view was an important part of apocalypses. Maintaining a sense of urgency is still an important part of appreciating the apocalyptic message. Seeing the end as near rather than as distant keeps the matter of living for God urgent. The time "is" near.

THE LETTER OPENING
(1:4-8)

The letter opens in the typical way with an identification of the sender and the recipients, a greeting, and a doxology. The greeting follows the pattern found in the letters of Paul: grace (*charis*, a modified form of the usual Greek greeting *charein*) and peace (from the standard Hebrew greeting, *shalom*). But the identification of the source of grace and peace is itself suited to the message of Revelation: they are from "him who is and who was and who is to come, and from the seven spirits who are before his throne." God is identified as the one who embraces all time. In a sense, this is like standard Greek attributions of gods, especially Zeus, but with a significant difference. God's eternity is described in terms of action: "He who is to *come*." As we see later, the one who is to come is Jesus. This is an early indicator that Jesus is the one who reveals who God is. The seven spirits, who are also the source of the grace and peace greeting, are identified by John elsewhere as angels who are under the authority of both God and Christ.

The greeting is also from "Jesus," who is identified here as the Messiah (Christ), but also with titles that John uses to draw a close connection between Jesus and the original readers. He is "the faithful witness" (*martys*), one who was, as were the readers, called to be faithful even unto death. He is "the firstborn of the dead"—the first but not the last! The readers too have a hope for resurrection. He is also "the ruler of the kings of the earth," in contrast to the Roman emperors who claimed to be such. In comparison to Christ, their claims are proven to be empty. These attributes of Jesus are in a sense to be shared by the readers. In 2:13, Antipas is also called "the faithful witness." The readers are called to be faithful witnesses as well. They have the hope of their own resurrection, and they will have a share in the rule that Christ will bring.

The greeting is followed by a brief doxological prayer (vv. 5b-6). Paul used such portions of his letters, usually cast as a thanksgiving, to indicate what some of his major themes would be. So does John. The doxology is addressed to Jesus, who has made the readers' redemption possible. John subtly reminds the readers that they needed redemption. He does not just depict the world and its powers as evil. Even Christians are in need of forgiveness. Jesus has accomplished that already through his death and has made it possible for Christians to fill the role of being "a kingdom of priests," a role that Israel was to have filled (Exod 19:6), but which John says has now fallen to the church.

The doxology flows into John's initial prophetic pronouncement (v. 7). Here he sounds out his basic message of hope. The one who first came in obscurity will come again in triumph, and there will be no mistaking his power. Words from Daniel 7:13 and Zechariah 12:10 are blended here to give them a new interpretation. John uses Old Testament prophetic words, but he is not bound by their original meaning; he gives them new life. The reference to coming "with the clouds," taken from Daniel, also recalls the vision of the coming Son of man in the book of Enoch, a popular Jewish apocalypse used by early Christians. Zechariah's words about wailing were originally restricted to the inhabitants of Jerusalem, but John expands them to include all the earth.

The conclusion to the opening of the book (v. 8) draws on Isaiah 44:6: "I am the first and the last; beside me there is no other god." John expresses the same thought using the first and last letters of the Greek alphabet, alpha and omega. Jews often referred to keeping the whole law from *aleph* to *tau*, their first and last letters. John then quotes the passage itself. The thrust is that God is the beginning and end, and therefore in control of all history. The phrase "Lord God . . . Almighty" uses the most complete name for God found in the Old Testament, in the form in which it appears in the Septuagint, where it reads "Lord God of Hosts." Thus, it depicts God as in control of all powers.

FIRST MOVEMENT
THE PRESENT EXPERIENCE OF PILGRIMS
(1:9–3:22)

THE INITIAL VISION
(1:9-20)

John's letter now begins to follow the narrative form that we generally see in apocalypses. The narrative here focuses on the present experience of faithful pilgrims, both the recipients of the letter and the author John. He identified himself as one who shared the experience of those to whom he wrote. He specified three things they shared: (1) persecution (literally, "tribulation," from *thlipsis*, a term often used to denote eschatological suffering), used here to mean those trials they have already faced and those to come as the End approaches; (2) kingdom, a future reality that is already being experienced by those for whom Jesus is Lord; and (3) patient endurance, the character of Christians who live in the intervening time when Jesus has become Lord to them and the time when he actualizes his lordship over all things. They shared these things "in Jesus." Their common identity stemmed from their connectedness to him.

John wrote that he was on the island of Patmos "because" of the word of God and the testimony of Jesus. Patmos was not a penal colony, but Romans sometimes put troublesome persons there. It had a fortress, a famous school, and pagan shrines to Artemis and Apollo. The connection of the place with Apollo allowed John to draw on certain parts of the legends about this deity later in his book. John's identification with his readers' trials would support the idea that he was there because of his previous preaching.

He was "in the spirit," a reference to the spirit of prophecy that came upon him "on the Lord's day," probably referring to Sunday since this was the time of Christian worship. If so, this is the earliest Christian reference to Sunday as the Lord's day. It could mean Easter or the eschatological day of the Lord, but probably not. The time he received his prophecy was the time when his readers were also gathered in worship.

He was commanded to write, a typical feature of apocalyptic literature, and to send his writing to the seven churches. To communicate the meaning of what he saw, he wrote drawing on Old Testament images and other symbols that would have been meaningful to his readers.

John's initial vision is a glorious one. He sees seven golden lampstands with "one like the Son of Man" in their midst. He later explains that the lampstands are the churches to whom he writes. The one like the Son of Man calls to mind both Daniel 7:13, where it seems to refer collectively to faithful Jews, and to 1 Enoch 37–71, where it refers to a heavenly figure who comes to save the righteous and judge the world. It also points to those eschatological teachings of Jesus about the coming Son of Man. The long robe is like the priestly garment of Exodus 28:4, and the golden sash/girdle appears in 1 Maccabees as the royal emblem of the king. The white hair is like that of the Ancient of Days in Daniel 7:9, and the description of his feet and voice recall the angelic messenger of Daniel 10:6 (cf. Ezek 43:2).

The cosmic magnitude of the vision is indicated by the "seven stars in his hands." The parallels to this are not in the Old Testament but rather in the cult of the emperor and of the Zoroastrian god Mithras, who became popular with Roman soldiers. Generally, the seven known planets were viewed as heavenly beings with power. Seven stars sometimes appeared on Roman coins, signifying Rome's power. Claiming that Christ holds the stars was a challenge to astralism and to the emperor cult. The stars do not hold human destiny, nor does the emperor embody cosmic rule. Christ commands both.

His only weapon is a sword in his mouth. Isaiah 11:4 says the deliverer of Israel will smash the enemy with "the rod of his mouth." Isaiah 49:2 says the "Servant" had a mouth like a sharp sword (also that he hid his people in the shadow of his hand). His weapon is his word; he acts through speaking, just as God did in the very beginning.

John's response to this vision is to be overwhelmed, like Isaiah and Ezekiel. But the same hand that held the stars touched him and revived him. Christ appeared to communicate, not dazzle. He revives John reminding him that he (Jesus), too, had been dead but lived and is the living one. In fact, he "holds the keys of death and Hades." Hellenistic mythology said that Hekate held these keys and directed the traffic between the other world and this one. The text affirms that death is under the control of Christ; it does not lord it over his people.

John is again told to write; that is his job. He is to "write what he has seen." Then, he is also to write, "what is and what is going to become." This could refer to three things: (1) what you have seen now, that is, the vision of chapter 1; (2) what is, that is, the letters to the churches; and (3) what is to come, that is, the message contained in chapters 4–22. But both chapters 2–3 and chapters 4–22 move between past, present, and future. It is better to take the phrase as referring to the book as a whole or to the act of seeing: write what you saw, both what you see right now and what you are going to see later.

Part of the mysterious vision is explained: the lampstands are the churches, which by implication have a role to give light, to bear witness. The stars are explained as the angels of the churches. This could mean guardian angels; it probably means the heavenly counterparts to the earthly congregations who represent them before God. Earthly pilgrims are assured that despite their trials below, their lives are known to the Lord above.

THE LETTERS TO THE SEVEN CHURCHES
(2:1–3:22)

Having described his visionary experience, the author relates the message he has been charged to communicate to the faithful in the cities of Asia Minor. Each "letter" to the churches follows a similar pattern:

1. Identification of the addressees
2. A description of the attributes of Christ, based on the initial vision in Revelation 1
3. A statement of approval and/or blame related to what was actually going on in the church
4. A word of exhortation calling the church to be faithful
5. A word of assurance for the church

As a group, the letters follow the pattern of the prophetic oracle, especially as we see this pattern in Amos 1–2 where the prophet delivers pronouncements against six of Israel's neighbors and then one

against Israel itself. The beginning of each letter-oracle with the for-
mula "To the angel of the church at _____ write" is similar to Amos'
"Thus saith the Lord." Even though each oracle addresses particular
matters in the individual churches, the high degree of overlap between
them all indicates that in a sense all of the letters have a message for all
of the churches.

Ephesus (2:1-7)

Addressees. Ephesus was one of several Greek colonies in Asia
Minor, with the earliest settlement dating to the Mycenean period (ca.
1500 B.C.). Alexander's successor in the region, Lysimachus, relocated
the city (ca. 300 B.C.) to a more strategic site and began construction of
the famous temple to Artemis, which replaced an older building that
had already established Ephesus as a major site for worship of
Artemis. Three earlier temples to Artemis also were built there. Upon
the ascendancy of Augustus, Ephesus became the center of the
province of Asia. Additional religious structures to Roma and Julius
joined those already there. In the late first century A.D., under order of
Domitian, Ephesians built the first of their four Imperial Neocorate
temples, and Ephesus became one of the Asian cities that housed the
Koinon, an imperial priesthood that supervised the province's imperial
cult. Temples built to honor various other gods, goddesses, and heroes
also stood there. While Ephesus became the major center in Asia for
promoting the imperial cult, it continued to be most noted for its
temple to Artemis.

Description of Christ. The focus is on those attributes that stress
the transcendent power of Christ (stars in his hand) and his immanent
presence with his churches (walking among the lampstands).

Approval. The Ephesians are commended for their hard work and
enduring faithfulness in both verses 2 and 3. The Ephesians are also
commended for their opposition to false prophets, characterized as
evildoers and false apostles. In verse 6 the opponents are also called
Nicolaitans, a group otherwise unknown apart from Revelation. This
could be a group led by a person named Nicolaos, as later legend has it.
Or, this name could be John's own creation, as is Jezebel and Balaam
later, which he uses to characterize what appears to be the same
heretical group. Nicolaos could mean "conqueror of the people," which
is the Greek equivalent of the Hebrew name Balaam. It could just be a
description of their evil and deceptive domination over many in the
church. When John later mentions these people, he notes their
immoral behavior and commends the Ephesians for their active
resistance of such false teachers.

Blame. Nevertheless, the resistance to heresy has come with a
price, one that John considers too costly. They have lost the spirit of

love they had at first. The text has often been incorrectly read as referring to some "first love," with various interpretations of what that love was. Such readings miss the point: they had lost sight of the first thing, love itself.

Exhortation. The seriousness of losing sight of the "first thing"—love—brings out a warning: Repent and return to the priority. If they fail, they can expect the judgment of God. The exhortation section here also functions as a part of the approval part of this letter.

Assurance. The word of assurance is spoken by the Spirit, an indication that no sharp distinction is to be made between Spirit and Christ here. Images from Genesis and traditional apocalyptic ideas about Eden are used to speak of the promise of eternal life.

Smyrna (2:8-11)

Addressees. The ancient city of Smyrna, noted for its impressive walls and orderly design, had been depopulated by the Lydians around 600 B.C. The scattered Smyrnans retained their identity, however, and under Lysimachus a new Smyrna was built beginning around 288 B.C. Sometime around 195 B.C. Smyrna sided with the Romans against the controlling Seleucids and erected a temple to the goddess Roma. Writing early in the reign of Tiberius, Strabo called Smyrna the most beautiful city of all. Smyrna was one of the four cities in Asia recognized as a center for the provincial assembly and was also a Neokoros city, supervising temples in a large area. Around A.D. 155, Polycarp, bishop of the church there, was martyred. Since he was 86 when he died, he may have already been active when John wrote. A century later another Christian leader, Pionius, was killed. The powerful local Jewish population had a hand in Polycarp's death, according to the document "The Martyrdom of Polycarp," indicating that tensions between Christians and Jews here was severe over a long period. The Jews allegedly joined in charging Polycarp with teaching many citizens not to worship the gods. They are also described as helping to gather wood for his burning, even though it was on a sabbath.

Attributes. The aspect of the initial vision recalled has special relevance for Smyrna. The city had died and come back to life. Also, it later experienced the death of its Christian leaders, the threat of which had been real even in the first century when John wrote.

Approval. Smyrna was a wealthy city, but its Christian inhabitants did not share in that wealth. Furthermore, they were subject to harassment by the Jews who were in positions of influence. John labels these ethnic Jews the "synagogue of Satan"; they are false Jews.

Exhortation. The Lord does not promise to prevent them from experiencing hardship. They are told they will endure it. The affliction will be for "ten days," a short, but dangerous, time. The testing may be intended by their antagonist, the devil, or it may be intended by God as a way of confirming their faith. They are urged to remain faithful, even unto death. Later, Polycarp did just that.

Assurance. Judaism later developed more fully the idea of a second death, that is, the fate of those not resurrected to new life. Here, as later in 20:14, the second death is the ultimate judgment of God on the unrighteous. The faithful may suffer martyrdom, but they are assured that this is the only death they will endure, unlike the unfaithful.

Pergamum (2:12-19)

Addressees. In the third century B.C. Pergamum emerged as the center of a major kingdom in Asia Minor. Lysimachus had begun to fortify it by building a fortress on the steep acropolis overlooking the city. He left the treasures he placed there under his eunuch's supervision while he warred against the Seleucids. The eunuch took advantage of his absence to develop Pergamum's strength in the area and left to his brother, Eumenes, an independent kingdom. Eumenes' son, Attalus, proclaimed himself and his descendants king of an area that included large portions of what later became the Roman province of Asia. The Attalids aligned themselves with Rome, and upon the death of the last Attalid king, the whole kingdom was willed to the Romans. During the second century the Attalids greatly expanded the fortifications and other buildings of the acropolis and led the city to become a major architectural and intellectual center. The last Attalid king, Eumenes II, built an impressive temple to Zeus with a huge marble altar (now in Berlin). Some see this impressive structure as the throne of Satan John mentions, but most take John's reference to be the temple of Augustus, the first such temple built to an emperor in Asia Minor. John could have intended the whole acropolis, an imposing structure 800 feet high with a myriad of pagan temples.

The status of the city was diminished somewhat in the first century B.C. when Mithridates of neighboring Pontus overtook western Asia Minor and made Pergamum one of his bases for his war with Rome. The victorious Romans exacted a heavy price from Pergamum, and it was only in the first century A.D. that it began to regain some of its earlier prominence. One of the major centers of Asklepios, the Greek god of healing, developed there, leading to Pergamum becoming a major center for the medical arts. Despite the Christian congregation there, it remained a strong center of paganism even after Constantine legalized Christianity.

Attributes. The two-edged sword is the sword in Christ's mouth in the initial vision, his word of power. The sword could be an allusion to the Roman *imperium,* the power of the sword, of life and death. This power belongs to Christ, not to Rome.

Approval. They are commended for being faithful even in the face of death, as it had been experienced by one of their own, Antipas.

Blame. Though they have endured hardship, they have also been tolerant of heretical groups. These people are likened to *Balaam*, who is connected with the sin of Israelite men in the plains of Moab when they joined the Moabite women in eating sacrificial meat and engaging in orgiastic fertility practices. These are further connected to the Nicolaitans, again a name that may have association with Balaam. The opponents here seem to have a more lax view of accommodation to the surrounding paganism, permitting participation in the practices of the Pergamenes at large. In this, they reflect Paul's idea that eating idol meat of itself is not a sin. They do not follow Paul's lead, however, of refraining from such practice out of respect for others. Some see in them gnostic-like elements in that they are libertarian toward such fleshly matters. These persons hold that such acts cannot affect the spirit; John disagrees.

Exhortation. The call is to repent, but the warning is directed against the heretics. The warning signals that they should seek to be clearly distinguishable from those they now tolerate.

Assurance. The "hidden manna" may allude to the Jewish tradition that Jeremiah had hidden some of the manna in the Ark of the Covenant when the Babylonians destroyed Jerusalem. Some Jews held that this manna would be revealed in the last days. In contrast to the charge of eating idol meat, however, John may have intended a reference to God's provision of their needs, especially the provision of eternal life. As God had provided for the Israelites in the wilderness, even in the time of Balaam, God would provide for them in their struggle.

The meaning of the "white stone" remains unclear. It may allude to the use of such stones as magical amulets. Asklepian worship sometimes involved dedicating objects to the god of healing, often with the names of the worshiper on them and of their problem. Some note that such stones were also used as tokens for admission to athletic/social/business events. It may refer then to admission to the messianic banquet and would connect with the idea of the manna. Christians might be excluded from participation in the dominant cultural events around them, but they would share in full in the coming kingdom. Another view is to focus not on the stone but on the new name, noting ancient belief in the power of a name. The new name could represent the new identity of the believer or it could be the name of Christ to whom the believer belongs.

Thyatira (2:18-29)

Addressees. Thyatira was less prominent than the other cities seen thus far, yet it was located at an important trade crossroads and was especially known for its wool industry. Inscriptions found there mention a wool-workers guild and dyers and fullers. From the inscriptions regarding trades, some have contended that trade guilds held prominent roles in the life of the city and that participation in these guilds, which would have involved communal meals and parties, led to immoral behavior.

An inscription in Thessalonica also mentions a trader of purple dye from Thyatira. Acts refers to Lydia of Thyatira as a seller of purple, a somewhat rare position for a woman. The concern with some local prophetess that appears below may reflect a setting where women were able to obtain a higher level of prominence than was customary in most parts of the ancient world.

Attributes. Inscriptions and coins from Thyatira indicate the city had shrines to Apollos and Helios, both of whom were often associated with the sun. Some see here an allusion to these gods in the imagery applied to Jesus who is depicted glowing as the sun. Perhaps. More likely the description picks up on features of Psalm 2, which is quoted below. There the focus is the destructive power of God's "son" over the enemy. This is the only place where John clearly speaks of the Son of God; it probably derives from his usage of Psalm 2.

Approval/Blame. Love is mentioned as the first work here. He also notes that their later works exceed their earlier ones. Unlike Ephesus, they have not declined in their practice of love. But there is much to blame, especially in regard to some local "Jezebel." Some contend that the prominence of Lydia in Acts indicates that in Thyatira women could rise to exceptional positions of influence, thus perhaps explaining why John attacks a woman in the church there, calling her Jezebel. Such a view holds that this woman has attained a position of dangerous heretical influence, even though she has been warned to repent.

More likely, John is again using Old Testament characters who were associated with leading Israel into idolatry as a way of describing the dangers of the heretical impulses in the church life there. Jezebel is the paramount representative of this in the Old Testament. Though Jezebel is not indicted in the Old Testament for actual fornication, she promoted Ba'al worship, which did involve fertility practices and which was often criticized by the prophets using the language of sexual immorality. Those who follow this loose approach to the Christian faith of joining in pagan practices can expect God's judgment.

Exhortation. The phrase "deep things of Satan" refers to teachings and practices advocated by the heretics. They probably did not consider themselves to be following Satan; they saw themselves practicing a form of Christianity that was not bound by normal scruples. They were free from the law and other human conventions that dealt with matters of the material world and not of the spirit. They were privy to the knowledge that such fleshly acts could not really affect their spiritual status, so unlike their more uninformed, conservative fellow

Christians, they could join in the culture around them without guilt. This attitude resembles the thinking of some later gnostic groups, but does not confirm that Gnostics actually existed in Thyatira at that time.

Assurance. John quotes Psalm 2:8, a royal psalm depicting God's granting of rule to his chosen one, his son. This "rule/authority" includes destroying the enemy. This rule is promised to those who overcome (conquer) in the present.

He also promises to give them the "morning" star, usually identified in antiquity as Venus, the symbol for Romans of sovereignty and victory. Thus, Roman generals said they owed their loyalty to Venus and built temples to honor her. Sovereignty and victory are to be given to the faithful followers of Christ.

Sardis (3:1-6)

Addressees. Sardis was a city of past glory. It had been the capital of the Lydian Kingdom, reaching its zenith in the sixth century B.C. Then, it declined into obscurity. Sardis had a supposedly impregnable acropolis fortress, yet twice it had been taken because of lack of watchfulness. Sardis also was a center of the woolen industry, including special dyes.

Later evidence from Sardis indicates that Christians and Jews seem to have tolerated each other well.

Attributes. The seven spirits and seven stars do not seem to be identical. The seven spirits are more like those seen later, and more like traditional Jewish views about seven works of the spirit, the first two of which were prophecy and quickening of the dead.

Approval/Blame. No clear approval appears, but a severe rebuke is clearly given. The church of Sardis has a reputation for being alive, but it is not really. Yet, the church is not completely dead. A few are acknowledged as having remained pure and unsoiled from the threatening influences. The language of corruption could be an allusion to its famous dye industry. The white garments here probably refer to the desired purity.

Exhortation. The appearance of death seems to be related to lack of diligence: no completed works! The reference to a thief recalls imagery found elsewhere in the New Testament (1 Thess 5:4). It also may allude to Sardis' past when the city was taken unexpectedly.

Assurance. The promise is available to the whole church there. The reference to the Book of Life mirrors Old Testament usage (Exod 32:32) where it also indicates those to be included in God's kingdom.

Philadelphia (3:7-13)

Addressees. Compared to most of the other cities addressed in Revelation, Philadelphia was relatively less significant. It was built by Attalus II and destroyed by an earthquake in A.D. 17. After that, it was never fully repopulated because people were afraid to live there. The impermanence of life there is contrasted in Revelation with life in the city of God. Pagan cults flourished there, but the church's problems seem to have come more from conflicts with Jews.

Attributes. The reference to the key of David echoes the earlier symbol of the keys of death. This key apparently opens the door to the kingdom of God and determines who enters. The imagery alludes to Isaiah 22:22 and the promise made to Eliakim who was to become king over the house of David.

Approval. Elsewhere an open door seems to refer to opportunity for mission work. Here, though, it seems to refer to entrance to the kingdom. Conflict with Jews or Jewish factions within the church lies behind the assertion that such opponents are not true Jews. The church, faithful despite hardship, constitutes the true Israel. Thus, the faithful ones will not experience the coming trial.

Exhortation. Those who hold fast shall receive a crown signifying victory and rule. The pillar image may be an expansion of the peg image in Isaiah 22:23. As an owner or builder of a building might inscribe his name on a pillar, the name on the faithful pillar signifies ownership by God. Here the idea of stability and permanence is stressed, unlike the earthquake-prone city.

Laodicea (3:14-22)

Addressees. The wealthiest city in Phrygia, Laodicea's success was rooted in banks, wool industry (black wool), and a famous medical school (known especially for its eye salve). Unlike its neighbors, Colossae and Hieropolis, Laodicea enjoyed sufficient resources to rebuild itself without imperial support following a devastating earthquake in A.D. 61. Its reputation for self-sufficiency was, thus, well known when John wrote.

Laodicea's location near a warm spring heralded for healing powers also figures into this message to the church.

Attributes. The depiction of Christ draws from Isaiah 65:16. The reference there to the truth of God is here applied to Christ. Thus, he is also the faithful and true witness. Casting Christ as the origin (beginning) of God's creation may allude to Proverbs 8 with its reference to wisdom as God's agent of creation, but it also expresses the same thought as Colossians 1:15-20, a letter that may also have been sent to Laodicea (Col 4:16).

Approval/Blame. No good word appears here. No charge of evil occurs either, only halfheartedness, which is considered worse than outright evil. The sickening quality of such halfheartedness is illustrated through allusion to the nearby warm springs and its sickening water. Furthermore, in contrast to the city's wealth, medicine, and cloth, the Laodicean Christians are poor, blind, and naked.

Exhortation. Here instead of an open door being given to the church, we find the church having closed its door to its lord who nonetheless knocks seeking entry. The image of door may allude to the Song of Songs 5:2, which early on came to be interpreted messianically by the church.

Assurance. To those who do respond to the call in Laodicea belongs the same promise of rule that is offered to other faithful witnesses.

SECOND MOVEMENT
THE INTENSIFICATION OF TROUBLES FOR PILGRIMS
(4:1–18:24)

THE THRONE OF GOD
(4:1-11)

Chapter 4 begins a new section that extends through chapter 18. An initial vision of God and the Lamb, which announces God's ultimate victory, is followed by seven seals, seven trumpets, seven bowls, and, finally, the fall of the Great City Babylon, which describes God's judgment. John stresses that the victory that comes at the end is already secured in the death and resurrection of Jesus. Salvation, then, is not something to be experienced in some eschatological future; it is already experienced in the historical present. From this point on, John does not focus on the faults of the churches to whom he writes; instead, he focuses on the church as a whole being faithful in its struggle against evil claims to lordship.

As is common in apocalyptic writings, John is caught up to a heavenly world where the true nature of things is revealed. In the Old Testament, prophets were sometimes depicted as being summoned before the heavenly council to hear the pronouncements of God. Even in chapter 10, where John appears to be back on earth, his view is still from the transcendent heaven. He is summoned to heaven by the same voice that spoke to him on earth. The exalted Christ and the earthly lord are the same.

John is to be shown "what will happen after this." He sees the one who was, is, and will be—the one who transcends all time. His vision is not to be only of a series of events to occur in the future, but a transcendent view of what always is and always will be. He is granted a vision of his own time, including his immediate future, from the vantage point of eternity.

In heaven John sees the throne room of God. This vision is central to the whole book. At the heart of all that happens, John beholds who is in control, the one who is made known through the lamb who suffers. His vision of God on the throne resembles Ezekiel's chariot vision: the throne itself, the thunder and lightning, the rainbow, the living creatures. Unlike Ezekiel, however, John does not see/describe the one actually sitting on the throne, except in general glorious images; instead he describes the lamb who defines the one on the throne. An important part of the vision is the counter claim to all worldly political pretensions, especially that of the Roman emperor who claims to be in control. John sees who is really on the throne of the universe. This one will bring judgment on all false claimants, but here at the start the rainbow is a reminder that the God who brings awesome and devastating judgment has made a covenant with the creation to sustain it.

The throne of God is surrounded by 24 other thrones; the rule is shared. Why 24? Perhaps this is an allusion to the 24 lictors who surrounded Domitian's throne. The 24 elders on the thrones place their crowns before the one throne, perhaps reminiscent of the Parthian king Tiridates placing his diadem before Nero in homage to him. Christians give their homage only to God.

The lightning and thunder coming from the throne are characteristic of theophany experiences in the Old Testament. Seven torches burn before the throne, representing the seven spirits of God, which were earlier connected to the seven stars and thus the seven angels. The imagery is fluid; it represents God's ministering presence and watchfulness over creation.

Just as the earthly temple in Jerusalem had a huge cauldron holding a sea, so does the throne of God. Both in the Old Testament and here the background is the Ancient Near Eastern mythic imagery of the watery chaos being subdued by God. Before God, the ever-threatening sea is placid, calm. In the new creation (21:1), the sea will vanish altogether.

The four living creatures on each side of the throne have details from Ezekiel 1 and Isaiah 6. They function as the traditional cherubim, a reflection of Ancient Near Eastern winged bulls or lions that guarded thrones. The four creatures represent the apex of the major orders of living things: eagle = birds, lion = wild animals, bull = domesticated animals, man = all creatures. Jewish tradition held that each of these creatures has sovereignty over a part of God's creation. Here it is stressed that all of them, including the man, are created by God. The creatures function here as a Greek chorus, singing out the dominant theme of a drama: God is the holy, eternal one.

The focus on created things may be in reaction to gnostic-like tendencies among some in the churches to discount the created world. Here the physical world is affirmed, and God is acknowledged as the creator. Pilgrims may have a final home beyond this world, but life in this world is not to be considered unimportant, nor is its significance to God to be ignored.

THE LAMB OF GOD
(5:1-14)

The closing part of the vision that opens the major section of Revelation includes much traditional apocalyptic imagery about the one who conquers in God's name. These images are reinterpreted, however, to give them a uniquely Christian character.

God on the throne holds in his hand the scroll that reveals the future. The angel's request for someone who is worthy to open this book and reveal its contents goes unheeded. So John weeps, because he fears that the future must remain unknown. But his weeping is interrupted by the angel's announcement that there is one who can open the book. He is the Lion of the tribe of Judah, the Root of David, and he has conquered, thereby qualifying him to open the book.

The "Root of David" derives from Isaiah 11:1, 10: "There shall come forth a shoot from the stump of Jesse, and a branch shall grow out of his root. In that day the root of Jesse shall stand as an ensign to the peoples; him shall the nations seek, and his dwelling shall be glorious." In apocalyptic literature this David-like messianic figure was a warrior who would overcome God's enemies.

The "Lion of the tribe of Judah" is an image that goes back to Genesis 49:9-10: "Judah is a lion's whelp." The apocalyptic works Testament of Judah 24:5 and 2 Esdras 12:31-32 understand the Lion to be the Messiah.

The stage is set then for the critical reversal of fortunes that God's people have been awaiting. They have been lambs led to the slaughter by the evil empires of this world. Now God's great Lion will come down upon them and set things right. But! . . .

What we now see is not a lion but a Lamb, a slaughtered Lamb, yet standing. This is not what the hopeful reader would have expected. This is where the conquering Lion is supposed to step in. Instead, we get a Lamb, and a little one at that, as the diminutive term *arnion* intends. The usual term for lamb in the New Testament is *amnos*. Only in John 21:15, Jesus' commission to Peter to "Feed my Lambs," do we also have *arnion*. The term is chosen carefully. The one who steps forward has been slaughtered, yet he has risen again to stand here before the throne of God. John has not described Jesus this way before. He has waited until this moment to reveal him as the risen, slaughtered Lamb who has conquered.

The use of the perfect tense for the word slaughtered indicates an ongoing reality. He was not just slaughtered at some moment in the past; his slaughteredness is a continuing reality. It is the fact of his death that makes him the conquering One. He did not come as the suffering lamb in the past and then assume the role of the warrior Lion for the future. He is still the Lamb who was slaughtered. That is how he conquered; that is how conquering is done, both for him and for the ones faithful to him. Conquering has a legal, forensic sense here. As did Jesus, the faithful Christians can expect conviction and execution from a court of Roman law; but their witness and acceptance of death constitute their conquering, or acquittal, in the only court that really counts, the heavenly one.

The beings around the throne acknowledge that the lamb was slain and thus is worthy to open the scroll. They begin the new song of praise that is eventually sung by all of God's creatures. The four creatures and the 24 elders sing the first and last verses. The song is taken up by the other residents of heaven. Then the whole of creation joins in the singing. There appear to be no holdouts, no part of creation that remains in rebellion ultimately. "And the four living creatures said, 'Amen!' And the elders fell down and worshiped." The final word of acknowledgment comes from those around the throne.

THE SEVEN SEALS
(6:1–8:1)

Chapters 6–18 constitute the bulk of Revelation and primarily consist of a triple series of eschatological woes depicted in terms of seven seals, seven trumpets, and seven bowls. The first two series are interrelated and follow a definite pattern. The first four elements in each series form a group of related catastrophes. Then the next two in each group depict an intensification of the eschatological distress. These are both followed by an interlude, which in turn is followed by the seventh element in the series. After an extended interlude in chapters 12–15, the final series of woes occurs, which culminates in the destruction of the Great City Babylon.

In the depictions of eschatological woes, traditional imagery from the Old Testament, especially that associated with the plagues on Egypt, is combined with allusions to political and religious entities that were a part of the Greco-Roman world in which John lived.

The First Four Seals: The Four Horsemen
(6:1-8)

The famous Four Horsemen of the Apocalypse initiate the woes with typical apocalyptic usage of images related to war, plague, and death.

They portray the judgment of God on human claims to power, especially as it was embodied in the Roman empire.

The First Horseman. The rider on the white horse armed with a bow would have immediately evoked in the readers' minds the dreaded fear of the Parthians on the eastern border of the empire. Only the Parthians had mastered mounted archers, and white horses were their trademark. The Romans never conquered the Parthians and had experienced several devastating defeats at their hands. They stood as the ever-threatening end of Rome's claim to earthly dominance. The announcement that they were on the march was a signal to Rome of its impending downfall.

Later, John will describe another conqueror on a white horse, Christ himself (19:11-16), who will actually bring the end of Rome's rule. The first white rider is a pale premonition of the one who is to come. This one rides out in violent military conquest; the one who ultimately conquers does not do so through military might that kills but through the power of the Lamb who dies for others.

The Second Horseman. The second rider brings an end to the Roman peace and replaces it with anarchy.

The Third Horseman. The third black-horsed rider replaces Roman prosperity with famine. Food is rationed at 8-16 times the normal price; nevertheless the rich, those who have the oil and wine, continue to flourish.

The Fourth Horseman. The fourth pale green rider personifies the ghostly power of Hades and represents death in all its violent forms. Imagery from Zechariah, Jeremiah, and especially Ezekiel are used: sword, famine, pestilence, and wild animals.

The Fifth and Sixth Seals
(6:9-17)

The Martyrs. The fifth seal reveals one of the consequences of the great destruction. Those who are faithful to God in Christ will experience persecution and death. But from the perspective of heaven, their deaths on earth are like a great sacrifice poured out at the base of the heavenly altar of God. Like the Lamb, they have been slaughtered for their faithful witness, and like the lamb they are already in a sense there in the presence of God. But they are not smug; they cry out for relief for those who have yet to go through the bloodshed of martyrdom: "How long, O Lord?" In words reflecting Psalm 79:5-10, they cry out for God to reveal Himself and establish justice. Those slain are robed as victors and assured that the slaying of other faithful witnesses will continue only for a little while.

Cosmic Catastrophe. The sixth seal signals the expansion of distress to include the whole cosmos. In the traditional language of theophany John describes the coming of God's judgment. The inhabitants of the earth try to escape its coming, recognizing that it is the wrath of the lamb that was slain. Subtly John reminds the reader that the one who comes in judgment upon the world is the one who has died in behalf of the world.

An Interlude
(7:1–8:1)

The long interlude before the description of the end itself that should come in the breaking of the seventh seal depicts the sealing of God's servants. Instead of the expected end, we see the church triumphant. In contrast to the small numbers of Christians in local congregations that were struggling to survive in the face of Roman arrogance, we see the church depicted in grand size and stature.

The two images of the church that follow emphasize two dimensions of its life. First, the church constitutes the actualization of all the promises to Israel. Thus, the church is described as the completed Israel, 12,000 from each of the twelve tribes. The list of tribes does not match any Old Testament list, nor did most of these tribes still exist in any real sense in the first century. The tribes are symbolic of the fullness of God's people. What God began in Israel has come to its culmination in the church. The arrangement into divisions here also evokes memories of Old Testament passages that speak of Israel being arranged in military units. This is the church militant, at war in the struggle on earth against those evil powers opposed to it. Its weapon is faithfulness. Those who are engaged in the struggle below are sealed, not to be delivered from the struggle, even death, but delivered through it.

Secondly, the church is universal. It is the embodiment of God's relationship with Israel, but it is drawn from every nation. It is not ethnically determined. The scene now is heaven, after the battle, with the victorious servants of God. They are robed in white victor's garments, made white not by their own deaths but by the blood of the lamb. Now they enter into their eternal reward of peace and bliss for their faithfulness.

Silence descends in 8:1. Again, we are at the anticipated end. But first there is silence, a rather long one. As the first day of creation was preceded by silence, so is the day of the new creation. In other apocalyptic works, a deafening silence precedes the end. In the background are also the words of Zephaniah 1:7: "Be silent before the Lord God! For the day of the Lord is at hand."

THE SEVEN ANGELS AND THE SEVEN TRUMPETS
(8:2–11:19)

The Prayers of the Church
(8:2-5)

Before the next series of eschatological events, we return to see the ongoing worship in heaven. The church below also is at worship, perhaps wondering if its prayers are heard above. The description of worship here assures the church that its prayers are a part of the worship before the throne of God. This is John's pictorial view of the communion of saints. The prayers are heard and have an effect; things happen as a result. The kingdom prayed for will come, but not apart from the eschatological woes.

The First Four Trumpets
(8:6-12)

Trumpets were a part of temple worship below and are seen as a part of worship above. Jewish tradition associated the blowing of the last trumpet with the eschatological Day of the Lord. Like the first four seals, the first four trumpets here form a group. Here the eschatological woes are described in intensified fashion: for example, whereas before a fourth of the earth's inhabitants were struck, here it is increased to a third. By casting the events in language similar to Exodus, John stresses that God's action is both judgment and liberation.

The Fifth Trumpet: First Woe
(8:13–9:12)

Verse 13 puts the last three trumpets in a new key: they are specifically called woes. The vision of the fifth trumpet is cast from mythic images about the fall of the evil angel, seen in Canaanite mythology and reflected in Isaiah's denouncement of the king of Babylonia (14:4-20). While Isaiah's words originally did not focus on an actual fallen angel, later Jewish and Christian tradition made this connection. Some versions of the myth held that the evil angels were placed in a pit and would be released just before their final demise. John later adopts this motif in 19:11–20:15. John here uses the images to say that these evil powers serve God's purposes by inflicting the eschatological woes on the rebellious pagan world. The use of the passive voice ("was given") stresses that God is ultimately behind their activity; the evil powers are not sovereign.

Traditional locust-plague imagery, like that in Joel 1–2, is recast by John here. Unlike earthly locusts that attack vegetation and not humans directly, these diabolical locusts leave vegetation alone and attack people. Earthly locusts had no king, but these locusts have a king, a parody of Apollo, whose symbol was sometimes the locust and whose image was adopted by Domitian.

The Sixth Trumpet: Second Woe
(9:13-21)

John again elevates the Romans' historical anxiety about the Parthians to the level of eschatological symbol. The description of the vast attacking army from the East uses elements of Parthian appearance, but makes them demonically bizarre.

Despite the horrors of these plagues, the people harden their hearts as did Pharaoh and do not repent. Just as faithful Christians refuse to "repent" of their faith when persecuted, the Roman world refuses to turn away from its false worship and worship the creator.

An Interlude
(10:1–11:13)

As the interlude in chapter 7 focused on two representations of the church (144,000, great throng), the interlude here depicts the church as prophets and martyrs during the time of the increasing persecution.

10:1-11 focuses on Christian "prophecy." The description of the descending angel is like the storm deity imagery used of Yahweh in the Old Testament. He also resembles the exalted Christ of chapter 1, indicating the transparency of the angel image to that of God and Christ.

In contrast to the scroll in God's hand in chapter 5, the one in the angel's hand is open. The scene is based on Daniel 12:1-10 and represents a revision of it: one angel instead of two, an open book meaning the time of fulfillment is at hand, and the period of half a septet indicating not a long period before the end.

Before this end is revealed, seven thunders sound, but John cannot write what he sees. His understanding is fragmentary. He does not know everything; only God does. Furthermore, God is not bound to the typical apocalyptic scheme wherein the final events must come immediately at this point. John's eating of the book is like Ezekiel's (2:8ff.); the message is bittersweet.

John is a prophet, but as Joel stated and Acts also affirmed, the spirit of prophecy was to be poured out on all God's people at the end. He depicts the whole church in its role as prophetic "witness." During the short period of persecution, the church exercises its prophetic witness, as represented by the two witnesses. The term for witness here, *martys*, does not yet carry the meaning that it would eventually have ("one who dies for the faith"), but the faithfulness of these witnesses unto death laid the basis for the later classical sense of martyrdom. The faithful witnesses are killed on earth but raised up by God and vindicated. John draws on the imagery of Zechariah 4, where the reference is to Joshua and Zerubbabel. He applies it to the church, which is a community of priests and kings. When they are martyred, all nations view them, the church. They witness in a fashion like Moses and Elijah, two figures thought to have been taken up by God. Their power is evident only to the eyes of faith. They simply look like executed prophets to the world. The world thinks it has conquered them, but it has not. As in Ezekiel's vision of dry bones, God restores life.

The temple (church) is measured, marking it out for protection, as in the sealing of the church earlier.

The Seventh Trumpet: Third Woe/Coming of the Kingdom (11:14-19)

The usual "one who is to come" is omitted because he is now coming. The coming of the final kingdom is also the coming of the last "woe," which is never explicitly identified. Justice and judgment do not seem to be as long-lasting as God's grace and mercy. Here John does not hesitate to describe the end, but he does so in only general terms. The explicit description will come in chapters 19–22. He gives a tantalizing vision: the Ark of the Covenant, which was expected by many Jews to reappear at the end.

THE STRUGGLE WITH EVIL AND ASSURANCES OF VICTORY (12:1–14:20)

Chapter 12–14 constitute the theological center of the book. It is a unit that unmasks the real powers at work in the world and reveals the fate of God's faithful in triumph over those powers. It draws on mythic images from various sources and weaves them into a new picture. In particular, certain images that would have had special significance for the Romans are used to reveal the true nature of reality. For example, near Patmos lay the island of Delos, sacred to Greeks and Romans as the birthplace of Apollo. The evil dragon Python had tried to devour the infant Apollo when his mother Leto gave birth to him. Instead, Apollo slew Python. Roman emperors, including Augustus, Nero, and Domitian, adopted Apollo as their own deity and portrayed themselves after his fashion. For them, the goddess Roma had brought forth the emperor who conquered the powers of Darkness (so said the Roman poet Vergil) and established a new golden age.

In 12:1-6 John turns the imagery on its head. The Romans who saw themselves as instruments of light are actually the tools of evil. Behind their proud claims to legitimate power in the world lies that old serpent the Devil. They are his means for continuing his age-old struggle against God and God's people. But the Roman empire, or any empire that wills itself to power, is not the true power. God is, and God prevails, not through the power of death to others, but by experiencing death for others. The ungodly powers that be on earth give way to the power of God.

In contrast to Leto, Christians would have thought of Mary and the failed attempt of Herod to kill Jesus, the one who "rules" (actually "shepherds" all nations, rather than "breaking" them as Psalm 2 says in Hebrew). But more than Mary is intended here. It is the whole people of God, from whom the messiah has come forth. The messiah is snatched away and taken to heaven. But he was not snatched away from death, remember. He was saved "through" death and taken up to heaven. The end result is the casting down of the dragon from heaven. Not in some primordial time but in the earthly history of Jesus, in his life of engagement with the powers of evil and in his triumphant death, do we see Satan fall.

In 12:7-8 John describes war in heaven between the dragon and his forces and the army of angels led by Michael. Heaven is not the place where rebellion against God can be even temporarily successful, so the dragon and his army are soon dispatched.

But 12:9 and following show that while the dragon is conquered, he is not finished. He fights against his inevitable demise with full fury. He seeks a way to continue his efforts to destroy the woman, the people of God. He pursues her to the wilderness, where Israel was sustained by God after escaping from Egypt, and tries to overwhelm her as with the flood of chaos. But even the physical creation, long under the pain of earthly ungodly powers, exercises its inherent goodness and comes to her aid. So, unable to eradicate the people of God, to crush the church, the dragon goes after individual Christians.

How does the dragon do this? Chapter 13 says the dragon continues his rebellion by calling forth two other beasts, one from the sea and one from the land, reminiscent of Leviathan and Behemoth of old. Together they comprise an evil trinity. The dragon mimics God the creator, and like the primordial dragon of chaos of Ancient Near Eastern myth, he has seven heads and has a throne from which he rules. His beast from the sea is like Daniel's beast, representing a historical empire. 2 Esdras shows that by John's day, Jews had come to see the Roman empire as an embodiment of this beast. John's readers would also have seen the Roman empire in this beast, and John makes the identification even more explicit in chapter 17. The heads of the beast bear blasphemous names, asserting divinity, as the emperors did on their coins and elsewhere. One of the heads bears a mortal wound, probably recalling Nero's death by stabbing himself in the neck, yet he was still believed by many to be alive. The beast is alive and well and active in the Roman empire, trying to kill the faithful. In many ways the beast mimics Christ, receiving its power from another power, the dragon, as Christ did from God. The beast also reflects the image of the dragon as Christ reflects the image of God.

The sea beast that arises from the sea invades the land, as did the Romans invading Asia Minor, and summons another beast to aid it on land. This beast also mimics Christ in that it has some resemblance to a lamb. But it speaks with the voice of the sea beast. It is a false prophet, and in this respect mimics the role of the Spirit that speaks a true word of prophetic witness through the faithful. Like a false Elijah, this beast calls down fire from heaven and does other signs that deceive people into worshiping the sea beast whom the land beast represents. While the sea beast is political, the land beast has the trappings of religion. Hence, it could have been seen as embodied in the indigenous koinons and communes that promoted the emperor cult in Asia Minor. It could also have been embodied even in the members of the churches who advocated accommodation to the cult. It reflects the false word of all religious efforts toward making the dominant cultural view the true religion (God and Country). It thrives whenever and wherever human empire is idolized.

The worst act of the land beast is to mark/seal the people of the earth, claiming them as its own and lording it over them, manipulating the means of economy and politics to promote the worship of the sea beast, which is ultimately the worship of the dragon. It marks them with the mark of the (sea) beast, the number 666, a number of judgment and incompleteness. The mark is designed to be a mark of power, but it is an evil power, the power that is opposed to God. The mark on the head and the hand is a parody of Deuteronomy 6, in which the word of God is to direct thought and action. John's readers would have probably seen here a veiled reference to the persecuting power of Rome first experienced under Nero. But the symbol is more than Nero. It reveals not who any particular person is but "what" they are. They are of the devil. They are opposed to God and God's people. And they receive the judgment of God.

John is not so much concerned to reveal who the offending parties are—his readers already knew who was persecuting them. He is concerned to reveal the evil power that is behind this and every act of aggression against God. As Ephesians 6 states: "We are not contending against flesh and blood, but against the principalities, against the powers, against the world rulers of this present darkness, against the spiritual hosts of wickedness in heavenly places." John vividly portrays them in the garb of old images of chaos and evil.

John has exposed the earthly threats to the church for what they really are. He has unmasked their true identities and revealed what is actually happening. Now, in chapter 14, he reveals what is ultimately happening. The evil powers are at work against the people of God, but something else is going on in all of this. Those whom the powers that be are persecuting are sealed by God, and the powers themselves are being defeated even in their acts of death against the church.

14:1-5 recalls 7:1-8 and anticipates 21:1–22:6. Smeared by the blood of death, the faithful are really the undefiled, pure, truthful, virgins of God—the bride of Christ. Those who have died and those who have yet to die are proleptically already redeemed by the blood of the Lamb. Likewise, the powers that persecute them are already fallen, their fate also sealed by the blood of the Lamb.

The closing scene of this vision speaks of reaping. Because of the reference to the wrath of God and the blood flowing in 14:19-20, most interpreters take this to be a reaping for judgment. This view is reinforced by 13:9-11, which speaks of the torment of those who bear the mark of the beast. If so, 14:14-20 is another depiction of God's judgment on the oppressors of God's people.

Some, however, take 14:14-16 to be a reaping of the good harvest by the one like a Son of Man, thus the catching up of the faithful. They may then see the grapes being crushed as the wicked being judged, connecting it to the "wine of God's wrath" in 13:10.

Still, some see the crushed grapes also as the faithful, experiencing death "outside the city" as Jesus did. The persecution is a part of God's wrath, not directed as judgment against them, but a part of the eschatological woes that God inflicts on the earth, which includes the use of force by evil powers against God's faithful ones.

THE SEVEN ANGELS AND THE SEVEN PLAGUES (15:1–16:21)

This final series of sevens at last describes the end. It will be delayed no longer. This series is not to be seen as sequential to the other two, but rather a more intensive description of the same sequence. The final expression of God's wrath against evil's rebellion is provided by seven angels who possess seven plagues. But before the angels deliver the plagues of wrath the faithful who have passed through an ocean of fire, as it were, sing a song. In anticipation of the end and God's victory, the people of God are depicted in Exodus fashion as the Israelites on the far side of the crossed sea, listening to the victory Song of Moses (Exod 15). The focus of the song is not on destruction but on God. Everything that follows is set in this context of worship.

Then, the angels are given the means to dispense God's final wrath: seven bowls. The seven bowls are vials, like those used in the temple/tent ceremonies. The angels function here as the priests did. The bowls are like sacrificial offerings to God.

Chapter 16 describes the pouring out of the wrathful plagues from the bowls. As in the first two series, the first four bowls here form a unit. They depict cosmic disaster as various aspects of the created world are affected. This time, not just a fourth or third, but the whole earth is said to be affected. As the first four plagues proceed, there is a brief interruption after the third to remind the reader that what is happening is just. They are part of God's efforts to establish justice in a world where there is no justice.

The fifth bowl focuses on the political world as the wrath of God focuses on the earthly representative of rebellion. The sixth bowl resembles the sixth trumpet in that it speaks of a vast army from the East. The drying up of the eastern waters facilitates their attack.

The armies of the world are summoned by demonic spirits from the mouths of the unholy trinity in the shape of frogs. Why frogs? Partly because the sixth plague on Egypt involved frogs. Partly because Iranian religion held that frogs were the agents of Ahriman in the final contest in history. The frog-like spirits from the unholy mouths further represent a repugnant contrast to the "word like" a sword that comes from Christ's mouth. In the midst of these visions a warning about watchfulness goes out to the church from Christ. These visions are not to set schedules; they are to call the church to be faithful.

The armies gather at a place called *Harmagedon*. This is usually seen as a reference to ancient Megiddo where Israel saw numerous major battles fought. Since *Har* can mean "mountain," it is thought to be the tell on which Megiddo is located or Mount Carmel itself, which is nearby. Actually *Magedon* is not an exact match for Megiddo and may rather refer to an "assembly." If so, no particular place is meant. Even if it does mean the area of Megiddo, it is again symbolic.

The details of the end are not explored, only the result: the great city is devastated, along with the other cities of this world.

THE FALL OF BABYLON
(17:1–18:24)

The consequences of God's execution of wrath against the godless are now depicted. The reference to one of the angels with the seven bowls connects this vision to what has just been described. This is a closer look at what was going on during the seven-bowl series. Later the angel that introduces the descent of the New Jerusalem will be described similarly. This creates a great contrast between the Fall of the wicked city and the Descent of the heavenly city.

In the wilderness, the place of refuge for the people of God, they can finally see the great earthly city for what it really is, a harlot. Written on her forehead is the name "Babylon the great." All that Babylon represented for Jews as the destroyer of Jerusalem and the one who led Judah into exile, as well as all the paganism it propagated, is brought to bear here. Babylon is synonymous with the earthly kingdoms' proud pretensions to stand in the place of God. This harlot

Babylon sits on a red beast who is described similarly to the dragon and beast of chapters 12–14. This indicates that we have another vision of the same basic reality.

The Explanation of the Vision of the Harlot

The rest of chapter 17 explains what has happened. John was "amazed or confused" by the vision. So, the angel explains. John's readers would have connected this explanation to what they saw in their own time. The goddess Roma sat atop the Roman empire, beckoning people to worship the glory of empire. Verse 18 connects the harlot with the great city of Rome itself, sitting as the crown jewel of the empire. The empire is beastly when it threatens God's people. It had done so to the point of death in the past. It was not doing so at the moment, but it soon would. The seven heads are seven hills and seven kings, an immediate allusion to Rome's well-known topography and its leaders who are grouped together in a complete number seven. The readers live in the sixth one. Another is to come, indicating that the rule of this empire is not yet over. Attempts to identify particular emperors have all failed, and was probably not intended. They are a group.

Political powers in various places, ten kings, would direct their power against the Lamb-church for a little while, but would be overcome. Ultimately, though, the beast-empire and the other kings would turn on the harlot, the proud city. Evil is self-destructive, and God allows it to self-destruct. The destruction itself is not described. Despite its intense imagery, Revelation does not revel in the sufferings evil brings on itself. Instead, as we now see, there is mourning for the fallen enemies of God.

The Lament for the Great City's Fall

The end of the great city is announced in chapter 18 by an angel. Another voice calls the faithful to "come out of the city," that is, not to live according to its claims and demands. They are to recognize the higher, true authority of God.

Those who had followed the harlot lament her fall. They are amazed at its suddenness. This includes both political and economic power, kings and merchants and sailors, all of which benefited from her rule.

An angel also sounds the lament, and there is a touch of sadness that all the great activity that occurred in the great city is no more. It did not have to be this way. Earthly power did not have to exalt itself. The activities of the great earthly empire did not have to be self-serving. Human achievement is not the great enemy of God; claims to self-sufficiency and arrogance are. Babel's builders (Gen 11) erred not in constructing a city or tower, but in seeking a "name for themselves." Babylon, Rome, or any earthly power can exercise greatness as long as God is recognized as the true sovereign power. Self-exultation brings self-destruction, unfortunately.

THIRD MOVEMENT
THE FINAL VICTORY OF GOD FOR PILGRIMS
(19:1–22:5)

HEAVENLY PRAISE FOR GOD'S VICTORY
(19:1-10)

In the final movement the end is represented in seven scenes with each scene describing a different aspect of the end. Before the seven-fold depiction of the end, however, the heavenly crowd begins to sing in celebration of God's final victory. Here for the only time the word "alleluia" appears in the New Testament. It is the Greek trans-literation of the Hebrew "Hallelujah," which literally reads "praise ye Yah," with Yah generally taken to refer to the first two letters of the tetragrammaton YHWH, thus "praise the Lord." In the Psalms, Hallelujah is a word of direction to worshipers; it is not a part of their expression of worship. Here and in all later Christian usage, it is an expression of worship. The phrase "salvation to our God" also appears. It is a victory salutation. God has manifested what has always been true but what has been wrongly denied by earthly powers, that God alone is Lord and King. All other claims to such worship are now exposed as false.

Strangely, John, who has repeatedly insisted on worshiping God alone, bows down to the angelic messenger who announces the Beatitude on those invited to the Marriage Supper of the Lamb. The angel refuses to be worshiped. In Asia Minor, some Christians apparently had problems with angel worship (Col 2:14). This is a clear message for those who would focus devotion on the servants of the Lord rather than on the Lord.

SCENES OF THE END
(19:11–22:5)

The Lord's Triumphant Return
(19:11-16)

The first scene is the return of Christ. At this point John appears to be on earth again because he says he saw heaven opened. A rider on a white horse appears, as did one at the very beginning of the first series of sevenfold depictions of eschatological events. This horseman draws on several Jewish traditions. The Wisdom of Solomon 18:15 describes God's judgment on Egypt in the Exodus as: "Thy all-powerful word leaped from heaven, from the royal throne, into the midst of the land that was doomed, a stern warrior carrying the sharp sword of thy authentic command." This is Jesus the Conqueror leading the armies of heaven. Militaristic imagery is used, but the method of rule is revealed in who he is. He is Christ the Lamb who wears a robe dipped in his own blood. He is the Word of God, and it is by the power of the sword of his mouth that he rules. His army consists of those whose robes are white, washed in his blood. He has the name that earthly emperors claimed: "King of kings and Lord of lords." He also has a name known only to him; he shares in the mysterious and unnameable being of God.

We are reminded here at the end that what is revealed is not an event or a thing but a person, one who is already known, Jesus who died as the faithful witness and Lamb.

The Last Battle
(19:17-21)

Ancient Near Eastern traditions typically depict a final battle in which the evil dragon of chaos is defeated. That imagery is in the background here. An actual battle is not described, only the results. The battle has in a sense already occurred, in the cross. Two groups are defeated: the beast and false prophet, the culprits behind the rebellion of the earth's peoples, are captured and thrown into the lake of fire. The rest, the kings and captains, the mighty and the horse riders (with their horses), the free and slave, the small and great, are all killed by the sword, the word, and consumed in a mass feast that parodies the marriage feast of the Lamb. Two feasts are held, one for the church and one for those who oppose God and God's people. These are the only two options given. Zephaniah 1:7-9, which is itself a reworking of Ezekiel 39:17-20, is also in the background. Those who thought they were to be the guests turn out to be the menu. The contrast of feasts depicts the good celebration of receiving God's grace and the horror of rejecting the Creator.

Satan's Binding and the Final Defeat
(20:1-6)

John's sevenfold vision of the End continues, with each vision characterizing the End in a different way. Two parts of this End are the binding of Satan and the Millennium.

Satan Bound (20:1-3). In the preceding vision, Satan's earthly agents were removed. But what about the evil reality behind them? First, this evil will be overpowered; then it too will be destroyed.

John uses motifs familiar to the apocalyptic tradition. Iranian religion also spoke of the evil serpent being chained up at the end.

Isaiah 24:22 speaks of the powers of evil being locked up in the Pit. 1 Enoch, Testament of Levi, 2 Peter, and Jude also depict this motif, though in different ways.

Evil is brought under control so that it no longer deceives the nations. They too, though instruments of evil, have been victims.

The release of Satan that comes at the end of this scene is not described until later in verses 7-10. Why is he released? Evil is persistent. But it is conquered in the end. Dualism is not eternal. God is ultimately in control. In reality, evil has already been conquered in Christ. But now, this victory is seen only by the eyes of faith. Ultimately, it will be apparent to all.

The Millennium (20:4-6). Christians have the assurance of eternal life beyond the grave, but God's salvation involves more than this. It has a cosmic dimension. The earth must also be freed from the power of evil. Hence, God's rule through Christ is established on the earth.

While the millennium has received much attention, it is only a small part of John's total vision. Here, it is one of the several ways he depicts the significance of the End. Other apocalyptic works also had such a period of earthly bliss at the End. They differ in describing its length. Here it is the longest of all periods in Revelation, indicating the grandeur of it compared to other times. Its presence here reflects John's blending of two eschatological traditions. Old Testament prophetic eschatology envisioned the coming of God's kingdom within history. At that time, God's people would assume their rightful places of priestly rule. Apocalyptic eschatology affirmed the coming of the End from "beyond" history. A transformed earth and heaven would arrive. John affirms the Old Testament prophetic view of God's salvation within history. The millennium is a part of the historical activity of God. But he also later affirms the apocalyptic End. God brings in a "new" heaven and earth. This cosmos is ultimately transformed.

Here in the millennium, the faithful witnesses (martyrs) share in Christ's reign. They are those who have been faithful even unto death. Either John intends that only those who died are raised, or he intends the image to mean the whole church, both those who died and those who were willing. Either way, the faithful church is now triumphant. They have a priestly role, as the people of God were intended to have. Priesthood is a mediation between God and humanity. The priesthood is not self-centered, only enjoying its status. It always exists for the other. They also have a kingly function. They share Christ's rule. They are not ruled by evil powers. They are free in Christ.

John's discussion of the "first resurrection" can be taken to imply a second resurrection, perhaps the one described later in 20:12 when all the dead are raised. But these are not necessarily sequential events. They may be two ways of describing the same End. Then why a reference to "first" resurrection? Perhaps it was given in counter to the contention that the resurrection had already occurred. The Pauline and Johannine letters attack this view. Some believed, perhaps because of ecstatic experiences that they had already been resurrected, hence the first resurrection. John may be asserting that the "first" resurrection has not yet occurred.

The description of the millennial reign of Christ and his faithful witnesses is bracketed by the closing line of the scene of the binding of Satan and the opening line of the scene describing Satan's last stand: "After that he must be let out for a little while," and "When the thousand years are ended, Satan will be released from his prison." The logical question to raise here is Why. Why must Satan be released after a while?

One way to answer this question is to say God "must" do it this way. There are constraints even on God that require that it happen this way. This approach raises a difficult theological issue. It makes God subservient to the eschatological scheme. 2 Esdras understood that this was so. That apocalyptic work says that God would like to have saved more of the creation but was unable to do so. God had to follow the script of a rigid theological system that could not be violated. Mark 13:20, however, affirms the sovereignty of God over the eschatological drama. God changes the schedule; God shortens the days of tribulation for the sake of the elect. God is not bound. Revelation 10:4 could also be interpreted as an indication of God changing the plan: The seven thunders speak, but God intervenes and will not let what they say be written down. It will not happen. Again, God is not bound.

The question arises: Is God ever bound? Must God do certain things, or are there things God cannot do? In his book, *When We Talk about God, . . . Let's Be Honest*, Kirby Godsey writes (99): "God does not abolish evil and suffering because God cannot abolish evil and suffering. . . . God suffers with us, and the mantle of suffering becomes the power of a new creation." But Godsey is not talking about the ultimate triumph of God; he means our experience of the working of God in the midst of life as it is now.

Another way to approach the issue is to see John bound, not God. God is not bound to release Satan, but John is constrained by his apocalyptic traditions. He has to tell the story this way. The apocalyptic tradition in which he stood had already developed the idea of an intermediate period when the goal envisioned by prophetic eschatology would be realized; that is, the messiah would establish an earthly kingdom. But his apocalyptic tradition also envisioned a higher goal, that of a truly eschatological kingdom that would transcend this earth, that is, the new heaven and earth that he will describe later.

John is also constrained by the fact that he seems to be following the script of Ezekiel here in these closing chapters. Ezekiel 37 describes a resurrection and the establishment of the restored king-dom of combined Israel and Judah. Ezekiel saw God returning all the Jews from all their lands and establishing them finally in the promised land. John's vision of the millennium in which the faithful witnesses are raised to rule on earth with Christ expresses this conviction.

Ezekiel 40–48 also has a vision of the divine reconstruction of the city of Jerusalem and its temple. It is his crowning vision. In Revelation 21, John follows this scheme with his description of the new Jerusalem coming down from heaven.

But before John can move to Ezekiel 40–48, he has to do some-thing with Ezekiel 38–39 and the vision of Gog, who is the ultimate manifestation of evil rebelling against God. Ezekiel 38–39 influenced nearly all apocalypticism with its graphic depiction of the final battle between God and evil. But since for John the ultimate source of evil is Satan, he must be released from prison to deceive the nations of the world. Gog cannot work apart from the influence of Satan. John is bound more by a literary necessity than by a theological one.

The Defeat Of Gog and Magog: Satan's Last Stand (20:7-10)

Except for the fact that Satan once bound must be released for this scene to take place, this vision is not to be seen as sequential to those before it. It is another of John's graphic portrayals of the End. John here depicts the End in terms of God's overthrow of Gog and Magog. While Ezekiel spoke of Gog of the land of Magog, Jewish tradition had long since transformed the one entity into two, Gog "and" Magog. John does not intend actual historical nations here; that is why he draws on imagery that is bigger than life. These images convey the sense of the ultimate confrontation between good and evil. This is evil's last war cry, though in the end it is only a whimper.

Evil surrounds the people of God, who are depicted as a camp. The camp is the beloved city. The camp imagery expresses the idea that God's people are a pilgrim people with no lasting home. As we have seen before, evil tries to destroy the people of God, but it will fail.

As in 11:17-19 and 19:17-21, no great battle is described. The ene-mies are quickly consumed by fire, and the devil is thrown into the lake of fire. It is all over. Evil is gone. No battle need be described, because it has already occurred in the cross.

The Final Judgment (20:11-15)

This scene is the only judgment scene John describes. It is another vision of the end. John is describing the same reality, but not in terms of supernatural forces. He is focusing on humanity and its role in the cosmic drama. Great powers are at work behind the scenes, but ultimately they are visible in the affairs of persons. Persons may have been the victims and the pawns of evil, but they are accountable. Human activity is to be taken seriously. Saying the devil made me do it, even if true, is not sufficient. We stand responsible for our actions.

This vision indicates that all the dead are intended, not just those who have done evil. As in a courtroom, the record books are opened. They contained the recorded deeds of humans, all that they have done. Another book also is opened, the one that contains the names of those who are to receive life. The sentence is given by the one on the throne who is not described. He is never described, apart from how he is seen in Christ, the Lamb.

Death itself and Hades, the abode of Death (or, more exactly, the ruler of the house of death), give up their dead, that is they release their hold on them. They have no more power. They are destroyed. And those who are not in the Book of Life are also destroyed, all thrown into the same lake of fire to which the beast, the false prophet, and the dragon-Satan have been disposed.

The New Heaven and Earth
(21:1-8)

Again, the cosmic dimension of God's rule is asserted. All creation must be liberated from the suffering of evil's tyranny. God's victory results not only in success over the enemy but more importantly in the transformation of that (those) for which God has exercised dominion. Here the creation of a new heaven and earth provide the setting for the final description of existence experienced under the full rule of God: life in the new Jerusalem.

The descent of the holy city is a grand, climactic moment in the drama. Violence, bloodshed, anger, and wailing have characterized the drama thus far, both as it has been experienced by the faithful of God and by the forces of evil. Now, almost in anticlimactic fashion, peace and quiet accompany the majestic arrival of God's full presence with the creation. The God who makes all things new has subdued all opposition and offers a life of bliss to those who through faithfulness have arrived at their appointed destination.

The New Jerusalem
(21:9–22:5)

Numerous sources existed for the imagery John uses to describe the New Jerusalem. In fact, the idea of a heavenly Jerusalem as the ultimate home of the people of God is not new to John. Galatians 4:24-31, Philippians 3:20, and Hebrews 11:10; 12:22; and 13:14 all use heavenly-city language to speak of the destiny of Christians.

The concept was already there in the apocalyptic tradition they inherited. Its elements are found in various Old Testament and extra-biblical apocalyptic passages. Consider, for example: the descent of a city established by God (Pss 46, 48; Isa 2:1-4; 65:17-25; 1 Enoch 90:29; Syb Or 5:420-25), God's throne (Ps 47:8; 1 Enoch 24:4-5), seeing the face of God (2 Esdras 7:98), the tree of life (Test Levi 18:11; 1 Enoch 25:5), gold and jewel construction (Exod 25:5-14, 17-29; Isa 54:11-14; Ezek 28:11-17; Tob 13:16-18), golden streets and gates of pearl (Isa 60:11-14; Tob 13:16-18), jewels for the walls (Exod 28:17-21; 39:10-14; Ezek 28:13; Josephus and Philo), the perfect cube of the Holy of Holies (1 Kgs 6:20; 2 Chron 3:8-9). The idea of the perfect city is also found in secular sources: various Hellenistic/Roman descriptions of the ideal city; Herodotus' description of ancient Babylon; Rome's proud claim to be the Eternal City, as depicted on coins. But above all, John is using the description of the new Jerusalem in Ezekiel 40–48. He has followed the scheme of Ezekiel in chapters 37–39, and now he draws from Ezekiel 40–48 for his final vision. Yet John weaves all these elements into a distinctive picture that transcends all of them.

A Description of John's Holy City. The city is the crowning jewel in John's description of the new heaven and earth. The old heaven and earth have passed away; all that remains is new. And the sea is no more. Revelation 21:5 stresses that God is making "all things new," not that God is making "all new things." Here we see a transformation of what has been, not a complete and total new creation but a recreation.

The new Jerusalem comes down from heaven and appears as a bride, picking up on Old Testament imagery that depicts Israel as the bride of YHWH and New Testament references to the church as the bride of Christ. John specifies the city as the bride of the Lamb. God is always seen through the Lamb.

The city radiates with God's glory; the city and the glory of God become indistinguishable. The city has four walls, each having twelve gates with the names of the tribes of Israel on them. They face the East, North, South, and West. The walls have twelve foundations bearing the names of the twelve apostles. The walls are a perfect cube, each dimension of incredible size: 12,000 stadia (1,500 miles); 144 cubits for the walls also is a multiple of twelve.

The wall is made of jewel jasper. The twelve foundations radiate with twelve jewels, as did the breastplate of the high priest, which both Josephus and Philo associate with the zodiac. The traditional correlation of stones with constellations shows that John gives them in reverse order here, thus making a statement about the zodiac being superseded in Christ. The twelve gates are made of huge pearls, and the streets of transparent gold.

The city has no temple, no sun, no moon, no closed gates, and nothing accursed. The city is the temple; God is everywhere present.

The Lamb is the light, and there is no darkness. The gates are always open to the outside, and people may always enter, but not everyone. The river of life flows through the center of the city, reminiscent of Eden and of Ezekiel's vision. Likewise, the tree of life is there, as in Eden and in Ezekiel.

In the city there is no more curse. Nothing bears the curse, first seen in Genesis 3. In 21:8, John detailed who was excluded: the cowardly, the faithless, the polluted, the murderers, the fornicators, the sorcerers, the idolaters, and all liars—all who have been guilty of compliance with the false claim to power of the beast, especially the cowardly and liars, those who were not faithful. The throne of God, the Lamb, is there, and his servants eternally serve and reign.

The Significance of the Vision of the New Jerusalem. Foremost, it is John's vivid depiction of the reality he has seen. It is another one of the ways he has woven various traditional elements together to try to express what he has seen. The picture he paints is not what he has seen; it is his communication of his vision. We should avoid mistaking the portrayal of his vision for what he actually saw. He was trying to communicate the reality the only way it could be communicated, in picture language drawn from his theological tradition. The language is metaphor, as is all theology. It is our only way of talking about God.

John is talking about God . . . and God's people. Here at the end, after all that has been described in the prelude to the End, what we see is God with God's people . . . so intimately "with" God's people that they live "in" God, in a radiant, glorious, almost unimaginable existence. No temple representing God is needed, or possible here, because God is the total reality in which God's people live. God, seen in the Lamb, is the light of their lives. John stresses that God is with God's peoples (plural, 21:3); the number is vast, as is the size of the city. They are no exclusive elitist group, though they do not include those who have deliberately turned away from God. Such is the final destination appointed for faithful pilgrims.

THE POSTLUDE
(22:6-21)

THE CLOSE OF THE VISION
(22:6-17)

After the final vision of the heavenly Jerusalem, John's attention is drawn back to earth, where the faithful must still meet the challenges of worshiping and serving in the face of great dangers. Two final themes emerge from this closing section: (1) "Worship God" and (2) "I am coming soon."

"Worship God." The final vision was one of the saints worshiping God in the new Jerusalem, but the saints on earth cannot wait until the End. They are to worship God, and God alone, now. The emphasis on worship to God alone is seen in John's third mistaken attempt to worship the angel of the vision. Neither the agent of the vision nor the vision itself are to be worshiped, only God. (Neither the preacher "nor the book" should be worshiped!)

The sixth beatitude of the book is pronounced upon those who keep the words of the prophecy of this book (21:7). "Keeping" the words is like keeping the sabbath, that is, living obediently to the will of God, as expressed in the book's call to faithfulness.

"I am coming soon." The stress on Christ's coming is made seven times in the closing verses (vv. 7, 12, 17, 20). The point is also made that the time is near (vv. 6, 7, 10, 12, 20). For that reason, unlike other apocalyptic works, John is told not to seal up the book. Other apocalypses try to give the impression that they were written in times past and preserved until the proper moment to be read. Not so for Revelation; the indication is given that the time is "now." Verse 11 gives a new slant to the similar close of Daniel's vision in 12:9f., which reads: "The words are shut up and sealed until the time of the end. Many shall purify themselves, . . . but the wicked shall do wickedly; and none of the wicked shall understand." The Septuagint renders this "until many purify themselves, . . . and the wicked do wickedly and fail to understand." John's language reflects that he understands those days to be at hand. Evil is rampant and does not recognize the lordship of Christ; only the righteous see the truth.

The "I" who is coming soon is Christ, the one who has been revealed as the victorious lamb of God. He is also to be revealed as the judge. In Revelation 20:13, judgment was related to the Lord on the throne. Here it is related to Christ at his coming. The End is the one who was in the beginning.

The seventh and last beatitude, in the form of an acquittal, is pronounced on those who "wash their robes" (in the blood of the lamb). They shall share in the redemption of Christ. They shall receive life in the heavenly city, but not those engrossed in the world.

Verse 16 reminds the readers of the source of this revelation. Verse 17 repeats the invitation that is still standing to heed the Lord's call and enjoy the water of life. In the end, the Christ who triumphs over those arrogant foes who appear as such a threat to those who would be faithful, softly woos his children.

JOHN'S LAST WORD
(22:18-21)

The book ends as it began, as a letter. As with the letters of Paul, the intention is that the book will be read when the faithful are gathered in worship, which typically included the eucharistic meal in which the presence of Christ was invoked. The one who comes to them in worship, in the breaking of bread, is the one coming in triumph.

A typical apocalyptic curse is threatened against any who tamper with the book's message. They shall have no share in the tree of life. The right to the tree of life here at the end repeats the first promise given in the letters to the seven churches. And, it signals the final restoration of that gift that was denied in the Garden of Eden.

The last word of the book is a word of grace from the Lord Jesus to all. Some old manuscripts read "to all the saints," or "all your/his saints," but the oldest simply say to "all." Here, at the end of the glorious vision of the victory of the sovereign God and the destiny of faithful pilgrims, a victory won through the death of the Lamb and a destiny to be experienced even in the midst of death, travelers on the way are assured of the grace that makes the journey possible.

FOR FURTHER READING

Beasley-Murray, G. R. *The Book of Revelation.* New Century Bible. Greenwood SC: The Attic Press, 1974.

Boring, M. Eugene. *Revelation.* Interpretation. Louisville KY: John Knox Press, 1989.

Caird, G. B. *The Revelation of St. John the Divine.* Harper's New Testament Commentaries. New York: Harper & Row Publishers, 1966.

Fiorenza, Elisabeth Schüssler. *Revelation: Vision of a Just World.* Proclamation Commentaries. Minneapolis: Augsburg Fortress, 1991.

Metzger, Bruce M. *Breaking the Code: Understanding the Book of Revelation.* Nashville: Abingdon Press, 1993.

Reddish, Mitchell G. "Revelation." *Mercer Commentary on the Bible.* Macon GA: Mercer University Press, 1995.

_____. *Revelation.* Smyth & Helwys Bible Commentary. Macon GA: Smyth & Helwys Publishing, Inc., 2001.

Smith, T. C. *Reading the Signs: A Sensible Approach to Revelation and Other Apocalyptic Writings.* Macon GA: Smyth & Helwys Publishing, Inc., 1997.

Thompson, Leonard L. *The Book of Revelation: Apocalypse and Empire.* New York: Oxford University Press, 1990.

Wainwright, Arthur W. *Mysterious Apocalypse: Interpreting the Book of Revelation.* Nashville: Abingdon Press, 1993.

ALL THE BIBLE

AREA	TITLE*
Genesis–Deuteronomy	*Journey to the Land of Promise*
Former Prophets	*From Promise to Exile*
Latter Prophets, excluding Postexilic	*God's Servants, the Prophets*
Poetry, Wisdom Literature	*The Testimony of Poets and Sages*
Exilic, Postexilic Books	*The Exile and Beyond*
The Four Gospels	*The Church's Portraits of Jesus*
Acts of the Apostles, Epistles of Paul	*The Church's Mission to the Gentiles*
Hebrews–Revelation	*The Church as a Pilgrim People*

*subject to change